The Historic Oakland Cemetery

of Atlanta

SPEAKING STONES

Cathy J. Kaemmerlen

Charleston  London

THE
History
PRESS

Published by The History Press
Charleston, SC 29403
www.historypress.net

Copyright © 2007 by Cathy J. Kaemmerlen
All rights reserved

Cover images by Eric and Robert Gaare.

First published 2007
Second printing 2009

Manufactured in the United States

ISBN 978.1.59629.330.4

Library of Congress Cataloging-in-Publication Data

Kaemmerlen, Cathy.
The historic Oakland Cemetery of Atlanta : speaking stones / Cathy J.
Kaemmerlen.
p. cm.
Includes bibliographical references.
ISBN-13: 978-1-59629-330-4 (alk. paper)
1. Oakland Cemetery (Atlanta, Ga.) 2. Atlanta (Ga.)--Biography. 3.
Atlanta (Ga.)--History--Anecdotes. 4. Atlanta (Ga.)--Buildings, structures,
etc. 5. Historic sites--Georgia--Atlanta. 6. Sepulchral
monuments--Georgia--Atlanta. 7. Epitaphs--Georgia--Atlanta. I. Title.
F294.A862O25 2007
929'.509758231--dc22
2007031630

To my dad, Cyril Joseph Kaemmerlen,
July 13, 1921–May 10, 2003.
To live in hearts we leave behind is not to die.

Photo by Eric Gaare.

Contents

Contents

Contents

Acknowledgements

I would like to thank the following people, without whose help this book would not have been possible: David Moore, executive director of Historic Oakland Foundation; Mary Woodlan; Kevin Kuharic; Davant Turner; Penny Hart; George Hart; R.B. Coulter; Larry UptheGrove; Mendel Romm; Sperry Wilder; Rosalind Hillhouse; Kathy Vogel; Elizabeth Garges Izard; Patricia Scheff; the staff and docents at Oakland; the staff at the Kenan Research Center; Dr. Mark Moran; Peter and Annette Mayfield; Elizabeth Sherwood; Pat McClure; Betty Anne Lynch; Jane Hinds; Bev Center; Susan B. Deaver; the entire staff at The History Press, especially Lee Handford and Hilary McCullough; the Genealogy Center and Archives of the William Breman Jewish Heritage Museum, Atlanta; Nathan Izzat at Alphagraphics; and last but not least, my son, Eric Gaare, and my husband, Robert Gaare, to whom I owe the most thanks of all.

Prologue

Most of us grew up thinking cemeteries are places to bury the dead. They are sad places, scary places, morbid places, places to avoid. Death is not something pleasant to linger over. It is not easy to accept finality.

My father, to whom I dedicate this book, did not have a "good death." It is still painful to think about it, some four years later. We watched him die over a period of months, watched him suffer one indignity after another. One treatment led to new problems, leading to another treatment that led to more problems. He had cancer that would not stop spreading. We were fighting a losing battle. In the end, we just wanted him to let go, to find peace.

The day he died I was hanging some wash on the clothesline. A gust of wind blew through, making the whirligig in his garden go like crazy. I felt so close to him then. It was as if he were still speaking to me, if I would only listen. It was a very comforting moment. We buried him in a typical modern cemetery, neatly manicured, with flat markers that lie on top of the ground to make it easier for mowing and maintenance. I have to remember that his plot is directly in line with the bench that is across from the mausoleum, or else I wouldn't be able to find it. All plots there look the same.

When I visit my dad and see his name, a rush of emotions and memories flood forth. He still speaks to me. He helps me to listen, to remember, to treasure. Now I realize that cemeteries are places for the living, places to go to find connections with the past.

Historic Oakland Cemetery in Atlanta is a Victorian garden cemetery and a vast historic treasure to the city and people of Atlanta. Oakland is full of beautiful speaking stones that tell us the stories of the past, of the people who came before us and helped to build Atlanta. Those who abide there are the silent witnesses of what has gone before. They are the links to the past. They remind us we are not alone, that we have all passed this way before.

They are the speaking stones, the voices from Historic Oakland Cemetery. Of the seventy thousand who dwell there, I am privileged to tell some of their stories. The stories that follow chronicle the story of Atlanta.

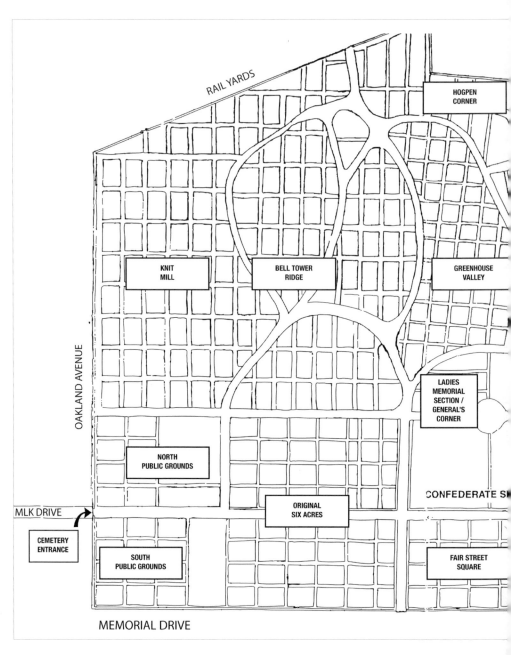

RAIL YARDS

HOGPEN CORNER

KNIT MILL

BELL TOWER RIDGE

GREENHOUSE VALLEY

OAKLAND AVENUE

LADIES MEMORIAL SECTION / GENERAL'S CORNER

NORTH PUBLIC GROUNDS

CONFEDERATE S

MLK DRIVE

CEMETERY ENTRANCE

ORIGINAL SIX ACRES

SOUTH PUBLIC GROUNDS

FAIR STREET SQUARE

MEMORIAL DRIVE

Design by Nathan Izzat.

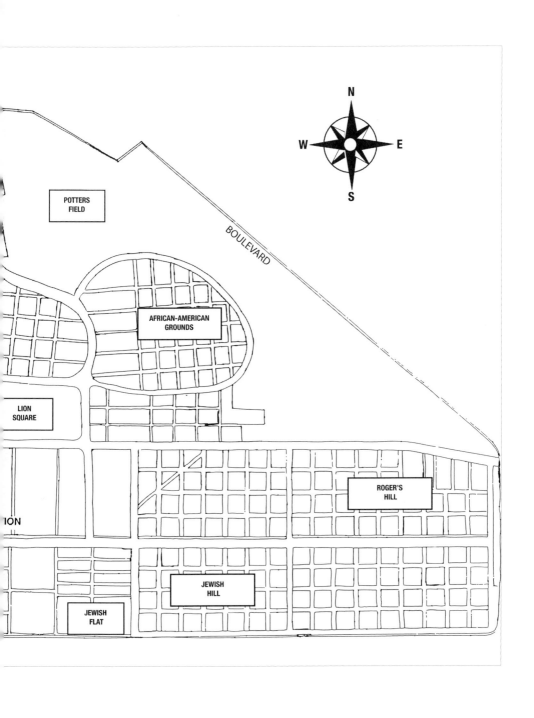

CHAPTER 1

Historic Oakland Cemetery

Oakland is the permanent home of many people who joined their lives with the city of
Atlanta. When we walk through the gates, we feel as if we are one with them.
—Jane Hinds, Atlanta storyteller

Historic Oakland Cemetery was founded in 1850 when Atlanta was just a country town of about 2,500 people. Its citizens were looking for a place to bury the dead. Pioneer citizen Reuben Cone gave one acre to the city and was willing to sell four adjoining acres of prime land within the city limits. But the city council instead voted to purchase land outside the city, reflecting a growing nationwide trend to place the city cemetery, with all its possible health hazards, away from the center of town. Alfred Wooding was willing to sell six acres of his "country land" for $450. It was a done deal. His original six acres became the city cemetery, or Atlanta Cemetery. Alfred's wife, Agnes, became the first occupant, as he moved her grave onto the grounds. Essentially everyone who died in Atlanta from 1850 to 1884 was buried here, making it Atlanta's richest historic site.

In 1872, the name changed to Oakland, and the area became the city's first park. Cast-iron benches and a growing number of oak and magnolia trees filled the grounds, which by then had expanded to forty-eight acres. In its heyday in the Victorian period, Oakland was described as the most attractive place in the city, where citizens congregated to spend a quiet Sunday in the park among friends and relatives, both living and deceased. It was not unusual for residents to pull up their carriage to the family plot, step out onto the specially designed carriage steps and picnic on the grounds and mounds and among the markers.

Oakland is a popular name among cemeteries, describing the spreading oak trees that provide shade and comfort for those souls who abide there in perpetuity. There are Oaklands in Arkansas (six), Florida (one), Illinois (four), Iowa (six), Louisiana (one), Minnesota (three), Missouri (two), New

The old and the new. A view of Atlanta's skyline and the Austell mausoleum. *Photo by Robert Gaare.*

York (three), Ohio (two), Pennsylvania (three), Tennessee (one), Texas (one) and even one more Oakland in Georgia. In Atlanta's Oakland, some seventy thousand souls have taken up permanent residence, with ten to fifteen new burials every year. But the cemetery is sold out, and has been since the late 1800s. Anyone wanting a spot at Oakland must be put on a waiting list, hoping a plot might become available. Occasionally this happens. Or if you're Maynard Jackson, former mayor of Atlanta, or Franklin Garrett, Atlanta's historian, room is made for you.

In 1976, historic Oakland Cemetery was placed on the National Register of Historic Places.

THE RISE OF VICTORIAN GARDEN CEMETERIES

To forget is vain endeavor, love's remembrance lasts forever.
Willie Young, only child of W.D.F. and B.A. Young, September 10, 1864–October 9, 1867

Oakland is a Victorian cemetery and depicts the garden cemetery movement that began with and is best exemplified at Mount Auburn Cemetery in

Massachusetts. The term "cemetery" derives from a Greek word for sleeping place. A typical garden cemetery is a welcoming place. Visitors find pleasant surroundings and a natural landscape, providing the right atmosphere for one to reflect upon life and death. Garden cemeteries are not places to shun the dead, but rather to honor them. Those interred have a comfortable resting place to wait for the rest of the family to join them and reunite in heaven.

A graveyard or necropolis, on the other hand, means a city of the dead. Early graveyards were frightening places, the stuff of nightmares and horror movies and devoid of trees, grass and flowers, with markers of skeletons and skulls. They were morbid places that were to be avoided, especially at night when Halloweenish ghouls and ghastly souls who had died too young, too suddenly or too violently would rise to punish the living. They sought their vengeance as zombies or creatures of voodoo magic.

The rise of Unitarianism in the early nineteenth century looked at death as a natural passage of life, as a reunion with nature (from dust to dust), not a horrifying final reckoning. William Cullen Bryant wrote in his *Thanatopsis* that death is "to mix forever with the elements." There grew an almost universal belief that families would be together in heaven just as they had been on earth. Death was just a different house for the family to dwell in. Tombstones were covered with warm comforting shawls, or made to look like cozy beds or resting pillows. They were decorated with symbols representing blissful slumber—poppies, cherubs, angels, lambs, roses. Married couples shared a common marker. Tributary words denoting the essence of the buried were inscribed in stone as a reminder to the living of this person's greatness of spirit. Oakland is such a cemetery.

Victorians thought it necessary to maintain one's class standards in death just as in life and, if possible, to use death as a means of further social advancement. If one could impose earthly patterns of living on the uncertainty of death, the deceased could assure himself of permanence and immortality. Buying a sizeable grave plot and constructing an impressive memorial to himself and his family would serve as a reminder throughout time that this was a person of power and status. The size of the grave marker forever indicates the power of males over females, adults over children and rich over poor. Oakland has fifty-five mausoleums and thousands of memorials and statuaries that honor the dead.

A Victorian Obituary

F.M. Coker, a wealthy Atlanta businessman and among the wealthiest men in the state in the early 1900s, was known for his efficiency, punctuality and being as "regular as clockwork." He died on September 13, 1905, and occupies one of Oakland's mausoleums. His obituary, or death notice, which appeared in the *Atlanta Constitution*, was a typically florid and descriptive one for Victorian times.

> *Last Wednesday Mr. Coker undertook to dress for the day. He had not been feeling worse, although the change in his condition became notable to his friends. When he stood upon his feet he fell and it was necessary to lift him back to his bed. Since that day he was slowly dying until the end came…Dr. Kendrick could do little more than stand by and watch the life of his friend ebbing away.*

CHAPTER 2

Founders, Early Pioneers, What's in a Name

So when a great man dies,
For years beyond our ken,
The light he leaves behind him lies,
Upon the paths of men.
—Henry Wadsworth Longfellow

THE NAMING OF ATLANTA

From 1837 to 1843, the small village at the end of the rail line of the Western and Atlantic Railway was known unofficially as Terminus. Georgia Governor Wilson Lumpkin was instrumental in the building of the railroad and securing, at no cost to the state, valuable land belonging to Mr. Samuel Mitchell that was located at the railroad's terminus. But it was time to change the name of this village, as it was growing in import as a valuable railroad juncture.

Governor Lumpkin declined the honor of having the town named after him, saying he already had a town and a county named in his honor. Mr. Mitchell would not hear of using his own name, and suggested the governor name the town after Lumpkin's firstborn child, daughter Martha. Thus Terminus became Marthasville and was incorporated by the state legislature with a post office.

However, the name Marthasville was too long, awkward on the tongue and sounded countrified. A man named John Edgar Thomson, who moved to Georgia when he was appointed chief engineer of the Georgia Railroad, suggested that the name be changed to Atlanta, the feminine form of Atlantic. The name would be in honor of the Western and Atlantic Railway and the termination point of the line from Augusta and the line from Macon. Much to the chagrin of Governor Lumpkin, who said his daughter had been robbed, the name was changed from Marthasville to Atlanta. The name stuck.

In a letter to his daughter, Governor Lumpkin wrote, "It would have been that name yet but for the predominating low voice of envy…The name being stolen from you will never change the facts." The story goes that when Martha was one year old, she displayed such activity that her father nicknamed her Atalanta, a goddess from Greek mythology known for her strength, fleetness and endurance. This name was added to Martha's name in the family register. The story circulated that the name Atlanta really came from Martha's middle nickname, Atalanta, given to her by her father, and somewhat adapted. Thus Martha Atalanta Wilson Compton went to her grave thinking the city had twice been named after her.

Jonathan Norcross, Atlanta's second mayor and a pioneer citizen, disputes this story as Lumpkin mythology and folklore. In a meeting of the Atlanta Pioneer and Historic Society in 1871, he said,

> *I recollect distinctly how the name of Atlanta was given to this city. It was formerly called Marthasville…I had a conversation with J. Edgar Thomson about it, and he said that he was going to call the depot Atlanta in connection with the Western and Atlantic Railroad. He did not care what they called the town, but he was going to call the depot Atlanta and the freight all came in marked Atlanta, and very soon the town came to be called Atlanta. It was not named after the goddess Atalanta and only the most ignorant people called it by that name…Atalanta had nothing to do with it.*

And so ends the saga of the naming of Terminus, Marthasville and finally, Atlanta.

WHO WAS ATALANTA?

Atalanta was the great Greek huntress, the daughter of Clymene and Iasus, who had hoped for a son. Iasus was so disappointed at the birth that he left his unwanted daughter to die on a hill near Calydon. She didn't die, but instead was suckled by a bear, raised by hunters and grew to womanhood. She participated in the Calydonian boar hunt, much to the dismay of all the male hunters, and even saved Meleager's life by killing a boar who was charging at him. As a result, she was given the prize at the hunt: the pelt of the charging boar.

The other hunters doubted that she had killed the animal. Her father was there to see her deeds and finally welcomed her into the family fold, but on condition that she marry, even though she had sworn to never do

Martha Lumpkin Compton, daughter of Governor Wilson Lumpkin. She has the honor of the city twice being named for her. South Public Grounds. *Photo by Eric Gaare.*

so. She agreed to marry the man who could beat her in a footrace. No one could beat the beautiful Atalanta, and one by one the men who raced her and lost were put to death for failing. Then Aphrodite stepped in, helping a man named Melanion to win. He was given three golden apples, which he dropped one by one during the race. Atalanta stopped to pick them up and that slowed her down enough so that Melanion won the race and the right to marry her. But apparently he forgot to be grateful to Aphrodite, so the two newlyweds were turned into lions for the rest of their lives.

> *I never saw more beauty than there was in the springtime in the groves all over Atlanta...The sward was covered with the fairest woodland flowers, floxes, lilies, trilliums, violets, pink roots, primroses—a fairer vision than any garden of exotics show now. Honeysuckles of every hue...The white dogwood was everywhere; the red woodbine and now and then a yellow Jessamine climbed on the trees. The streams were as clear as crystal. I have seen few things so fair in this world of beauty as were the Atlanta woods in 1848.*
> *—Recollections of an Atlanta Boy: 1847–1855*

Julia Carlisle Withers: Atlanta's First Baby?

She was called Atlanta's first baby, but when Julia Carlisle's parents, Willis and Sarah, came to the area on a warm day in June of 1842, the village was known as Terminus and was the terminating point of the railroad. Sarah White, just seventeen, had married Willis Carlisle, twenty-one, in Marietta, Georgia, in 1841. Reverend Josiah Burke, who performed the ceremony, advised the young couple to move to Terminus, as no doubt it was destined to be a large, thriving place. Being young, ambitious and with everything to look forward to, they took his advice. Judge Reuben Cone sold them a dwelling, an old commissary for road workers, but upon their arrival, they found it occupied by very stubborn tenants who refused to leave. Needing some sort of shelter, they found a dilapidated shanty that had last housed cattle, and camped for the night. Later on they found another shanty, little better than the one from their first night, but it became their home and place of business—a grocery store. Willis became the first merchant of Terminus.

Shortly after they settled in and set up shop, Sarah was about to give birth to her first child. But there was no doctor in Terminus. The closest doctor was in Marietta, so that's where Sarah was taken by stagecoach. Their firstborn, Julia, was born on August 17, 1842, and was forever known as Atlanta's first baby (although she was technically born in Marietta). When she was three weeks old, Julia was brought back to Terminus (soon to be Marthasville), and she lived in the area until her death.

In later newspaper accounts, Julia remembered the town of Marthasville consisting of a few shanties, with about one thousand people living in the town. Her mother was often lonely from the lack of friends. The streets were only dirt trails, with the tallest building being two stories with four rooms. Julia grew up living in a room adjoining the store until they moved to a house on Pryor Street.

Julia's mother was apparently responsible for the first fire in Atlanta. In those days, every woman did her own washing at the "wash house." You'd carry your soiled clothes to the wash house and drop them by the big pot boiling on the fire. One time when Sarah was visiting the wash house, she had to return home to tend to baby Julia. By the time she returned to check on the clothes, every garment the family owned was in flames. Willis took the stagecoach to Marietta the next day to "get a rabbit skin to wrap the baby bunting in."

Julia married Walter S. Withers, an Englishman, in 1862. He did not fight for the Confederacy; instead, he founded Withers Foundry and Machine Works and manufactured munitions for the Confederate army. The couple moved to Nashville when the Federal troops advanced into north Georgia. Some of the officers under Union General George H. Thomas were staying in the same boardinghouse where Julia and Walter were staying. (Of interest is the fact that Thomas was a Virginian who fought on the Union side. For being a turncoat, his family turned his picture against the wall and never spoke to him again.) When the Union soldiers found out where the Withers were from, they told them the city of Atlanta was gone, burned down. Julia retorted, "Well it may be gone, but you can't keep it burned down. It's like a cork on the water. It will always stay on the surface."

She later said she wished those officers would return to Atlanta to "view our streets and our buildings and our beautiful homes and see how true were my words," when the phoenix rose out of the ashes.

When Julia died on October 29, 1919, she was not only mourned by her many friends and family members; the entire city was bereaved by the death of Atlanta's first baby, who grew into a woman "cherished as one of the city's foremost pioneers." It was said she always had a deep and genuine love for her city. Her eight grandchildren served as her pallbearers.

She is buried in a special place in Oakland with a plaque to remind us all of her distinction as Atlanta's first baby. Her husband, Walter, preceded her in death. Her father died of typhoid fever in 1859, with his wife Sarah succumbing in 1898. All are buried at Oakland.

Note: Some say the first white girl born in Atlanta was Caroline Haas. There is more on her in the Jewish section in this book.

THE FIRST OAKLAND INTERMENT: AGNES WOODING OR JAMES NISSEN?

Similar to the dispute over the first baby born in Atlanta is the dispute over who was the first to be buried at the newly established city cemetery. When Alfred Wooding's offer to sell the city six acres of land for the establishment of a city cemetery was accepted in June of 1850, his wife Agnes had already died. Alfred kept a plot in the new cemetery and moved her body to its permanent resting place at city cemetery. Thus, she might have been the first occupant, but Dr. James Nissen is said to be the first direct interment there.

While visiting Atlanta in the fall of 1850 to attend a physicians' convention, Dr. Nissen took sick and died of pneumonia. Dr. Nissen had a fear of being buried alive, which was not an unusual fear for that day and time. Although the stethoscope was invented in 1816 by Theophile Rene Lannec from France, it was not widely known or used in America until much later. If Dr. Nissen knew

Agnes Wooding's grave. She was the first occupant of Oakland. Original six acres. *Photo by Eric Gaare.*

of and used a stethoscope, he did not entirely trust the results. He requested that before his body was placed in the ground, his jugular vein be severed, thus killing him if he wasn't already dead. The always dependable town doctor Noel P.P. D'Alvigny performed the throat slitting at the burial site.

Of note, Mary Todd Lincoln was also known for her fear of being buried alive. She requested "that my body shall remain for two days with the lid not screwed down." There was such a great fear of premature burials amongst the general public that coffin alarms were developed. One such alarm had a bell attached to the headstone with a chain that led down into the coffin to a ring that went around the finger of the deceased. Should the decedent wake up and find himself accidentally buried, he could pull on the chain and ring the bell in the cemetery yard and hope someone came to his rescue.

Dr. Nissen resides in the original six acres. His original marker is weatherworn, but a new memorial tells his story and his claim to fame as the first to be buried at Oakland.

MOSES W. FORMWALT: ATLANTA'S FIRST MAYOR

Moses W. Formwalt has the distinction of being Atlanta's first mayor, elected for a one-year term. (It was 1874 before Atlanta went to two-year

Dr. James Nissen's grave. He was the first Oakland interment. Original six acres. *Photo by Eric Gaare.*

terms, and then in 1929 to four-year terms with the right to succeed yourself for one more term.)

Moses was a self-made man, one of the few members of the new city's elite who came up from the ranks as a manual laborer. He was from Tennessee, of French descent. He settled first in Decatur and opened a tin and copper shop with partner John Adams in 1844. They dissolved their partnership in 1846, and Moses moved to Atlanta, living at the home of Dr. Joseph Thompson, who owned and operated Atlanta's one hotel. Moses reestablished himself in Atlanta with another tin and copper business, this time on Decatur Street. He distinguished himself in making and selling tinware and copper stills and sold them over much of the area, contributing to the growing number of whiskey stills and to the making and naming of the "Rowdy Party."

He was one of the "boys"—the Free and Rowdy Party boys—and he ran for mayor against the no-nonsense, pro-Prohibition, law and order candidate Jonathan Norcross. On Saturday, January 29, 1848, some 215 citizens cast their votes. Moses W. Formwalt was declared the winner. Apparently sixty fights erupted that day, much to Jonathan Norcross's dismay. Moses W. Formwalt was only twenty-eight years old.

After Moses's term ended, he continued to carry on his tin- and copperware manufacturing business, but took on a second job as deputy sheriff to Sheriff Thomas J. Perkerson of DeKalb County. On May 1, 1852, while escorting a prisoner from council chambers, he was stabbed to death. Thus he became the only Atlanta mayor to die from a homicide and the first DeKalb County deputy sheriff to be killed in the line of duty.

At the time of his death, Moses was one of only five men in Atlanta who owned as much as $20,000 in real estate, plus other personal items and four slaves. He was placed in an unmarked grave at Oakland and lay in obscurity for over sixty years until 1907, when the city council issued a resolution to provide an Oakland grave for Martha Lumpkin and to provide a memorial to him, Atlanta's first mayor. It took the city until 1916 to transfer his remains to his newly assigned plot and to construct a monument to his memory. He remains to this day in a prime spot near the bell tower and the fountain.

JONATHAN NORCROSS

When Jonathan Norcross became the fourth mayor of Atlanta in 1851 as a candidate for the Moral Party, he had his hands full. Three Rowdy Party mayors had preceded him, creating a town divided over law and order, with forty drinking establishments and a thriving red-light district.

The son of a clergyman from Maine, Jonathan was known as a temperance man who hated civic disturbances. He was told that if he was elected, he might find the town "too hot to hold him" if he executed his proposed reforms.

Not only was Norcross elected mayor, but he was also elected the chief of police and the superintendent of Atlanta's streets. He held the mayor's court and tried all the violators of municipal laws. His first offender, Allen Johnson, was a burly fellow who was found guilty and assigned a fine. The shock of a guilty verdict and an imposed sentence caused Mr. Johnson to draw a knife that was fifteen to twenty inches long and swear out loud that he'd make mincemeat out of anyone who touched him. He started slashing the knife in all directions to prove his intent. Mayor Norcross arose and used his split-bottomed chair as a shield and defense weapon. When the guilty knife wielder approached the mayor, the sheriff used a stout hickory cane to knock the blade from the offender. Johnson was seized and hustled out of the courtroom onto the street, where he escaped into the night. He was not apprehended.

Several nights later, Rowdy Party leaders, still upset over the election results, found a small cannon, mounted it on wheels and placed it in front of the mayor's dry goods store. They claimed they'd fire the cannon if he didn't resign. Mayor Norcross called a secret meeting of the city council and then called forth citizens to create a volunteer police force to help him enforce the city laws. Over one hundred men gathered, armed and equipped to fight if necessary, at the corner of Marietta and Peachtree Streets. They scared away the rowdy elements, captured fifteen to twenty leaders and put them in the caboose. The jail was far too small to house all the offenders. The backbone of the Rowdy Party was broken, with no more serious trouble thereafter.

Henry Grady, known as "the Father of the New South," dubbed Jonathan Norcross as "The Father of Atlanta" and as a "hard fighter in everything." Norcross demonstrated this quality from the beginning of his various careers and ventures, starting with his one-horse sawmill, with that one horse being blind but still able to provide the horsepower for the mill. Norcross foresaw Atlanta as the future gate city of the South. He died in 1898 and is buried in an unassigned grave at Oakland.

Dr. Noel Pierre P. D'Alvigny: Atlanta's Doctor

Born in France in 1800, Dr. Noel Pierre P. D'Alvigny served as a surgeon in the French army before immigrating to Atlanta in 1848 via Charleston. He became what many say was the prototype for Dr. Meade in Margaret Mitchell's *Gone with the Wind*. He was one of the most prominent doctors in Atlanta from 1848 until his death in 1877 (he was the doctor already noted as the one who slit the throat of James Nissen at graveside). He was also the good doctor sent for when Dr. Nathaniel Hilburn was stabbed to death by his brother-in-law Elijah Bird, and the good doctor who saved Atlanta Medical College from burning at the hands of General W.T. Sherman's Federal soldiers.

Atlanta Medical College, where Dr. D'Alvigny was an original faculty member, suspended classes in 1861 at the outbreak of the Civil War in order to serve as a Confederate hospital. When the city fell to the Federals and on the eve of Sherman's March in November of 1864, patients at the hospital were safely evacuated. The next morning, Union soldiers threatened to burn down the medical college. It was saved by a ruse of Dr. Noel D'Alvigny.

He plied the hospital attendants with whiskey, and they posed as patients in the hospital, occupying the beds. He demonstrated to the Union officer in charge that his hospital was indeed not empty, and took him to the beds where the attendants, on cue, began to moan and groan pitifully. Now how could the Feds burn down the hospital when it was still obviously occupied? After viewing the faux patients, the officer gave Dr. D'Alvigny until the next day to evacuate the wounded men. It was perfect timing, as the Federal troops pulled out the next morning, leaving the hospital and medical college intact. And there it stood until 1906, when it was torn down to make way for the building of the Atlanta College of Physicians and Surgeons.

The *Atlanta Constitution*, in an article on July 14, 1868, reported a serious illness of Dr. Noel P.P. D'Alvigny. "We are pained to announce the illness of this kindhearted gentleman and excellent physician." While performing an autopsy, he received a dissecting wound and failed to clean it until after the postmortem was conducted. The wound became infected and caused him to be in critical condition. However, he recovered and died in 1877, nine years later, and is buried at Oakland.

Among Dr. D'Alvigny's many honors is his commendation from the Federal government for taking care of sick Federal soldiers during the war. His son, Charles, followed in his footsteps as a noted physician and humanitarian.

THE FIVE LYNCH BROTHERS FROM COUNTY MEATH

There were five of them: Michael, the eldest; James; John; Patrick; and Peter, who was the youngest and came a few years later. They escaped the Irish potato blight and came to America in 1847. They came, as did many Irish immigrants, to escape famine and poverty in Ireland and to find work building America's railroads. As early as 1844, the DeKalb County Superior Court was busy issuing certificates of naturalization to Irish laborers to come to work on the railroads.

The industrious Lynches found their places and fortunes in Atlanta in the retail business. James started a grocery/produce business, promising that his prices were lower than those in Charleston and Savannah. John, Peter and Michael joined forces with James. Patrick was the loner, in the rock quarry business, starting a company that did well repairing Atlanta's cobblestone streets.

An early Atlanta credit reporter described the mercantile brothers as "having no business capacity but eternally industrious." He ate his words, as five years later the firm was worth a hefty $8,000. Then the brothers were classified and praised as "industrious and successful men."

By 1858 the business expanded to retail as well as a wholesale grocery business. The Civil War changed their expansions, temporarily. On record, none of the brothers fought in the war. Patrick reportedly weighed three hundred pounds and was not eligible to fight. When the war was over, Patrick traveled to Macon to defend the rest of his brothers, as men suspected of treason to the Confederacy. All suspected had to justify their cases. Patrick made a name for himself during the war when he

James Lynch's monument. He was one of the five Lynch brothers from County Meath, Ireland, who came to America to escape the Irish potato blight. Knit Mill section. *Photo by Eric Gaare.*

aided Father O'Reilly in asking General W.T. Sherman to spare Atlanta's churches. When the fires spread, intentionally or unintentionally to the churches, Patrick and his slaves formed bucket brigades to help put out the fires.

After the war, Atlanta became a boom town for the brothers, who were by then numbering four, as oldest brother Michael died in 1857. Patrick's rock quarry business contributed heavily in the rebuilding of downtown Atlanta until his death in 1871. John, James and Peter's mercantile establishment on Decatur Street was part saloon/part general store. Prominent Atlantans would stop by on their way to work to get their morning toddies, although there was no formal bar. Rare old brands of whiskey were kept in barrels on a table, with the rest of the stock kept in the cool basement. Each barrel had a faucet. Nearby was a water cooler. A customer would fill a tin dipper with water and then call for a drink. An employee would come to draw a drink from the barrel and the customer would put his money on top of the barrel. Thus explains the old saw, "Put your money on the barrel head."

Supposedly no customer was allowed to drink too much. But Pat Lynch McClure, a descendant of James, tells the story of the days when unclaimed property after the war was put up for auction on the courthouse steps. On those days, the Lynch brothers would offer free drinks at their saloon beforehand, making sure potential bidders and buyers had just enough to drink to make them slow to react. Then the brothers would outsmart the free drinkers and buy up the land. Pat says that's how the Lynches accumulated so much property in Atlanta.

You'll find the brothers buried on the large Lynch plot at Oakland, east of the bell tower. But if you ever visit the village of Slane, County Meath, Ireland, you'll encounter a weathered monument in an old graveyard erected by John Lynch of Atlanta in memory of his father Pat, his mother Nan, one brother Hugh and three sisters—Anne, Frances and Mary—who did not make it to America and died in 1849 during the Irish potato famine.

CHAPTER 3

From the African American Section

We will not go back, but forward...according to their light.
–Clara Maxwell Pitts

INTRODUCTION

Although Oakland is an inclusive cemetery, the Atlanta City Council ruled in 1852 that all blacks were to be buried in a specified section on the eastern boundary of the cemetery and could not be buried in the public grounds. By the time of the Civil War, some 869 blacks had been buried in this section; all apparently slaves. Approximately 60 percent were children who died of childhood ailments. Burial records during this time are incomplete. Oftentimes a black slave was listed by his first name with the term "Negro" afterward, or "slave." If a last name was recorded, it was the surname of the owner.

By 1860, there were thirty-one free blacks in Atlanta. Their occupations were restricted, and the opportunity for employment often depended on the benevolence of whites.

Post–Civil War there was a dramatic increase in the black population of the city. For many, their freedom from slavery was marked by disease and pauperism. Some became legislators in the carpetbag government before Georgia was readmitted to the Union and served under military law. Quite a few blacks rose to prominence as barbers, realtors, pastors, educators, dentists and social workers.

South-View Cemetery opened in 1886 for the black population of Atlanta. Still a significant number of prominent blacks were interred at Oakland. Several are featured in the section that follows.

Mary Combs: Free Black and Property Owner

Mary Combs was not only a free black woman in pre–Civil War Atlanta, but she was also a property-owning black woman. She was one of two blacks who owned property in Atlanta before the Civil War. Her lot was located at the junction of Wheat Street (now Auburn Avenue) and Peachtree Street. She paid $250 in "fee simple" on July 7, 1856, and sold the lot six years later to Lewis Scofield for $500. She had to have a white "guardian" to complete the transaction. Then, with the proceeds in her hand, she bought her husband's freedom.

After 1862, Mary and her husband are lost in obscurity. A Mary Combs is buried at Oakland in the black section, but her death is listed as April 4, 1877, with her age listed as thirty. If the records are correct and she is the same Mary Combs who bought her husband's freedom, she would have been nine years old when she first became a property owner, which is highly improbable. Could she have been the daughter of Mary and her husband? Since there was no such thing as a birth certificate for blacks in those days, there's not much reliability on the accuracy of the age of the deceased. Many records have a question mark for the date of birth.

Whatever the case, it remains a mystery what happened to Mary and her husband.

Augustus Thompson: A Blacksmith

He was born in Jackson, Mississippi, in 1837, the son of a freeman and a slave mother, Minerva Lee. With her four children, Minerva was willed to Mr. Julius Sappho of Madison, Georgia, in 1840, when Augustus was only three years old. His father could not accompany them. He was a freeman and if he moved to another state it would make him enslaved in his new state. So his father stayed free in Mississippi.

Although he was prevented an education as a slave in Georgia, Augustus learned the blacksmith trade, apprenticing for six years before he was declared a master of his trade. During the Civil War he made guns for the Confederacy. His skill was duly noted. While working in Augusta at war's end, he was declared a freeman and married Lorie Ann Jones. They were married for twenty-three childless years before her death in 1888.

Augustus moved to Atlanta in 1870 because Atlanta was a growing city, offering opportunities for hardworking free blacks. He opened up a successful blacksmith shop. It was said he never lacked for work.

Augustus Thompson's grave in the African American section. Note the anvil on top, denoting his pride in his skill as a blacksmith and founder of the Odd Fellows Lodge. African American section. *Photo by Robert Gaare.*

In 1870, the black population of Atlanta was 9,929. The opportunities were widening for former slaves who wanted to advance. The thirteenth, fourteenth and fifteenth amendments to the Constitution allowed blacks their freedom, their citizenship and the right to vote and run for election.

Augustus Thompson took advantage of his new rights and ran for city council from the Third Ward. He lost his bid. Although blacks were in the majority in his district, less than 40 percent of the men were registered voters. In 1868, white Democrats in Atlanta secured the general ticket system in an effort to keep blacks out of political office. This system called for at-large elections for all city offices. Fulton County operated with a white majority—Augustus didn't stand a chance.

Although Augustus was never elected to political office, he was a vibrant leader in the growing Atlanta black community and married his second wife, Katie, in 1889.

At some point in time, Augustus met James Lowndes of Louisville, Kentucky. James was a member of the order of Odd Fellows and, with the advice and help of James, Augustus established the first colored lodge of Odd Fellows in Atlanta, initiating twenty-five young African American businessmen into the lodge. More branches soon opened in Marietta and Dalton. The Society of Odd Fellows dates back to eighteenth-century England. It was considered "odd" for people to band together in an organization designed to aid those in need and to pursue humanitarian projects, thus the name.

Both Augustus and Katie are buried at Oakland. His grave marker is easy to spot. He has an anvil on his tombstone to denote forever his pride and success at being a blacksmith.

Ransom Montgomery: A Hero

Ransom Montgomery has the distinction of being the only slave owned by the State of Georgia, at least nominally, and the second black to own property in Atlanta. All this came about because he was at the right place at the right time and performed a heroic act.

In July of 1849, a Western and Atlantic passenger train carrying one hundred passengers was crossing a burning bridge over the Chattahoochee River. Ransom came to the rescue and saved all the passengers. The state legislature gave him his freedom, but really they were authorizing the state-owned Western and Atlantic Railroad to purchase him. Thus Ransom became the property of the State of Georgia. This was considered a proper reward for a slave who had saved a burning bridge and one hundred passengers on the passing train.

The State agreed to "provide him a proper home" and gave Ransom all the land lying near and around the Macon line roundhouse, thus making him the second Atlanta black to own property. In 1853, the chief engineer of the city railroads was authorized to pay him "a reasonable compensation for his services, so long as he shall continue to conduct himself in an orderly and proper manner."

On February 10, 1854, city council meeting notes record that "be it resolved that Ransom, slave belonging to the state, be allowed to sell coffee, cakes, etc. in the passenger depot for the accommodation of passengers." The city fathers still considered him a slave, although a privileged one.

Ransom was the brother of Andrew Montgomery, called Father Montgomery as he was a Methodist minister in the black community. At that time blacks were allowed to use the white churches for afternoon services after the whites vacated the premises. The two brothers were looking for a site on which to build a black church and called upon Colonel L.P. Grant (of Grant Park fame, and not buried at Oakland), who gave them a piece of land. The church was erected on this property but was destroyed by Sherman's "urban renewal project." After the Civil War, the land was taken from the black community, but Colonel Grant returned it to them. The Montgomery brothers sold this land and bought a more desirable piece of property on Wheat Street. The church that was built on this site became the famous Bethel AME Church, the first established African American church in Atlanta.

Ransom died in 1883 and is buried at Oakland.

ANTOINE GRAVES AND FAMILY

The Graves mausoleum is the only mausoleum in Oakland's black section. Antoine Graves was a prominent Atlanta realtor, onetime principal of Gate City Colored Public School and part of Atlanta's elite black society in the early 1900s.

He was married to Catherine Webb, daughter of Sinai Calhoun Webb, who had been born in 1830 as a slave and the biracial daughter of Judge William Ezzard and Nellie Calhoun. Nellie served as housekeeper and nursemaid to Dr. Andrew Bonaparte Calhoun, and upon his death she received a piece of property off the Calhoun Plantation in Newnan, Georgia. Catherine was born on this plantation.

Antoine and Catherine had six children. Two died in childhood. Lena Louise died in 1889 when she was nine months old; the cause of death was listed as laryngitis. Family folklore states that the singer Lena Horne,

The Antoine Graves Mausoleum, the only mausoleum in the Black section of the cemetery. *Photo by Eric Gaare.*

a cousin, was named for Lena Louise. Daughter Helen Lamar died of pneumonia at age twenty. Both daughters are buried at Oakland. Of the four surviving children, all attended college.

Antoine Jr. was a talented violinist. An August 1908 article in the *Atlanta Constitution* reported that at the age of twenty, having studied violin for twelve years, Antoine became a "violinist of significant attainment." He made his debut before a white audience to critical acclaim. The newspaper article remarked, "His art is characterized not only by real feeling and appreciation but a technique that is wonderful." He briefly toured Europe before studying dentistry at Harvard and setting up practice in an office on Auburn Avenue. His family nicknamed him "Judge."

Family patriarch Antoine served as the principal of Gate City Colored Public School (later known as Houston Street School) beginning in 1885. When former Confederate President Jefferson Davis died in 1889 and his body passed through Atlanta on the way to Richmond, the procession passed in front of Gate City School. Schools were ordered to close that day so all could attend the memorial parade. Antoine refused to do this, as he could not honor a man who had fought to keep blacks enslaved. To do this

Georgia Harris's grave. She was one of the two black women given permission to be buried with her white family. *Photo by Robert Gaare.*

he felt was contrary to what he was attempting to do at his school—uplift African Americans. Because of his refusal, the school board forced him to resign. He moved to California, returning to Atlanta shortly thereafter to open his offices in the all-white Kimball Building on Wall Street, where he became a prominent Atlanta realtor.

Antoine Jr. died three years before his father in 1938. It is said the father saved his son's ashes until his own death. Father and son were buried within a day of each other.

Two Blacks Buried in the White Section

Two white families requested that their black family "nanny" be buried in their family plots. Due to segregation restrictions for many years, the two families had to secure permission from the city council and from people who owned neighboring Oakland plots in order to bury their black servants with them.

Permission was granted in both cases. Catherine Holmes was the first to be buried, in 1896, in the Boylston family plot. According to family lore, she was never a slave. Her father's owner from Charleston paid him wages, which he saved until he could buy his freedom, his wife's and the children they had at that time. Catherine wasn't born yet, so she was born free. It was said she was a born storyteller and entertained her white charges with many legends from the Charleston coast.

Captain Isaac Boyd's family did the same for their servant, Georgia Harris. Captain Boyd was a successful Atlanta businessman who served in the Civil War. He died in 1904, sixteen years before Georgia died and many years before his wife Nannie Seawell died, thirteen years his junior. Georgia's exact birth date is unknown, but her date of death is listed in the Oakland records as being February 5, 1920. Her tombstone reads, "Georgia Harris—who born a slave, died the child of a King." The back of the stone reads, "In loving memory of our colored mammy."

CHAPTER 4

Murders, Suicides, Scandals and Tragedies

Oakland must be a magnet. It draws one back for more visits, as though the resting residents are calling out to have their stories told. You're never totally gone until all have forgotten you.
—Davant Turner, Oakland tour guide

AUGUST DENK: LOST AT SEA

German-born August Denk immigrated to the United States in the 1870s when he was only seventeen years old. Even before he set foot on American soil, he met an Atlantan onboard who was friends with Jacob Elsas, owner of the Fulton Cotton Mill. Procuring a letter of introduction from his shipmate, August became an employee of the cotton mill, studied English and was very popular among the workers. He rose from office boy to company treasurer, working at the mill for close to fifty years. The advent of World War I saddened Denk and his German-born wife, as they both had family members still living in Germany.

In 1918, August was to go to New York on company business, but his ruined nerves and bad health prevented him from going by train. His doctor recommended he travel by boat, as the sea air would do him good. No one could have predicted the tragedy that awaited him. On his return trip onboard the *City of Athens*, the ship collided with the French cruiser *La Gloire* in the early morning of May 1, 1918, off the coast of Delaware. Badly damaged, the *City of Athens* sank within seven minutes after the collision, killing 67 of the 125 passengers. Some of those 67 were killed when their lifeboat capsized. August Denk was not among the survivors. His marker at Oakland reads, "Lost at sea when the steamship *City of Athens* was sunk off the Delaware Coast."

CAPTAIN CHARLES WALLACE:
MURDERED AT WARRENTON

Captain Charles Wallace, son of Colonel Alexander M. Wallace, was murdered in Warrenton, Georgia, on March 12, 1869, by Dr. G.W. Darden in a crime of passion that snowballed in the press to a political one.

Charles, a battle-scarred veteran of the Confederate army, moved to Warrenton at war's end and became editor of the *Warrenton Clipper*, sometimes writing under the pen name Harry Percy. As a new member of the Warrenton community, he wanted to be accepted into the Masonic Lodge. Local doctor G.W. Darden promised to support Wallace's application, but he blackballed Wallace when the vote came up. Wallace retaliated by denouncing Darden in his newspaper, calling him a "liar and a scoundrel."

That's when Darden lost it. From a nearby second-story window, he watched and waited for Wallace to pass by, then fired multiple shots from a double-barreled shotgun, killing Wallace on the spot. Darden was immediately captured and jailed for his crime. That evening a party of men in disguise forced entry into the jail and into Darden's cell, took Darden away and shot him not far from the jail.

Northern papers picked up the story, assuming the "men in disguise" were Ku Klux Klan members who were retaliating for the murder of Wallace by lynching Darden, who was described in the Northern papers as a highly respectable and wealthy citizen. Wallace was described as the editor of a Ku Klux Klan journal. The *New York Tribune*'s article on the double murders concluded with, "How much longer must we wait for the organization of a legal and loyal legislature [in the South] that will pass laws to protect our lives and which the military, under order of a loyal President, can assist in carrying out."

This initial murder over a personal act of vengeance stirred up the still fresh animosity between the North and the South. Fair-minded journalism and a bit of digging would have revealed that both gentlemen involved in the murder were Democrats and were probably of similar political views. The question of which crime was the more heinous was not the real story.

Captain Wallace's body is interred at Oakland Cemetery in the family plot.

JAMES R. CREW: MURDERED,
BURIED AT OAKLAND, REBURIED AT WESTVIEW

James R. Crew was an upstanding Atlanta citizen who served as a railroad conductor and ticket agent for the Georgia Railroad and as a city councilman. During the Federal occupation, he served as an envoy between

Generals Sherman and Hood during the evacuation of Atlanta. Two weeks after the Federal troops left Atlanta to begin the march to Savannah, Crew fell victim to the desperate lawlessness of the times.

Three black men identified as Dennis Harris from Atlanta and two Macon friends of his, Henry Brown and "Bill," plotted to rob the ticket agent on his way home. On the night of the crime, Dennis Harris danced a jig at the railroad car shed, entertaining several hotel porters. Then he picked up a heavy iron bar at the railroad turntable and, with his companions, stalked James Crew, who left his office around 9:00 p.m. When he was only a short distance from the home of William Solomon, where he and his wife were boarding, Crew was struck by Harris from behind with the iron bar. Crew uttered, "Oh me!" as he fell. Henry Brown searched the victim's pockets and found a key. But it was not the key to the ticket office, where they hoped to find a goodly amount of cash. It turned out to be the key to the door of the Central Presbyterian Church, where Crew and his wife were members.

Crew managed to stagger to the front steps of the Solomon House and lived for two more days before dying from a fractured skull. He is buried at Oakland.

Sixteen years later, his wife remarried Colonel L.P. Grant, who was also widowed. He had a plot at the new Westview Cemetery. The new Mrs. Grant insisted her first husband be moved to the Westview Plot, as the first Mrs. Grant was already there. Grant died in 1893. Mrs. Crew Grant died in 1912 and is buried between her two husbands.

As for William Solomon, in whose house the Crews boarded, he too had a violent end, dying in 1874 from a fall from a window. He is buried and remains at Oakland.

THE HILL BROTHERS: FRATRICIDE AND SUICIDE

On November 26, 1886, R.P. "Bob" Hill, thirty years old, shot and killed his brother O.C. "Tony" Hill, thirty-six years old. Bob then shot and killed himself. Was it a fight over a girl named Kate Pinckney, whom they both loved, or just the result of too much drinking bringing out the worst in them? The *Atlanta Constitution* account of the shootings provided many lurid details and an answer or two.

The brothers were unusually close, even seen holding hands while walking down the street, two loving brothers—when sober. Apparently neither one was sober very often, and when they were under the influence they took on opposing personalities in true Dr. Jekyll/Mr. Hyde fashion. They were the only children of Colonel D.P. Hill, whose sister Ethel was married to

Jonathan Norcross, Atlanta's fourth mayor. The two boys were graduates of the University of Georgia, bright young men with fine, promising careers, Tony working with the railroads and Bob an attorney. They shared a room on the second floor of the Lovejoy Building, the lower part of which was once a saloon but had been vacant since Prohibition went into effect in Atlanta. Fulton County went dry on November 25, 1885. But that statute did not keep the brothers dry.

Their room was described as being neatly furnished with the basics. Closer inspection would have revealed bullet holes in the bookcase, evidence of previous drunken altercations between the two brothers. Events leading up to the murder/suicide seemed to reveal that great trouble was in the making. Tony Hill had been drinking for days, but on the night before the tragedy both brothers appeared relatively sober and in good humor. They had visitors to their room, where they played the banjo and guitar and sang gaily. They were both good musicians. Dr. Charles Pinckney (brother of Kate) was one of those visitors.

The brothers left their room that night, were seen together on the streets and by morning were both involved in their own agendas. Tony went to Dr. Pinckney's house and asked Miss Kate Pinckney to play the piano. She declined because there was no fire in the parlor. Tony replied, "Well, Miss Kate if you will play for me it will probably save Bob's life." She was the young lady the jealous brothers purportedly fought over.

Dr. Palmer remembered Tony visiting him later that day and said he was worried about his brother and asked the doctor for something to sober Bob up. He appeared to be delirious from the effects of alcohol himself and foreshadowed, "If Bob don't straighten up, something terrible will happen."

Bob returned home by that morning; two witnesses said he was intoxicated. He partially undressed and went to sleep. Around noon, Tony entered the Lovejoy Building and as he passed the street into the stairway, he met a friend. He told him, "I want to go up and straighten Bob out." That was the last time Tony was seen alive.

A fellow upstairs roomer, Mamie Johnson (Baker), heard four or five shots in rapid succession. She opened her door into the hallway. Another renter, F.B. Stanley, was coming up the stairs with a boy who was carrying his dinner. She shouted out to him that the Hill boys were shooting at each other again. She later reported that Tony had said to her a few days prior that "something will happen to Bob or to me. Some of these days we'll get drunk and kill each other. See if we don't."

With that thought on her mind, the two renters heard one last shot and then a heavy thud that sounded like a falling body. Mr. Stanley directed the boy to put down his dinner and go for an officer. Patrolmen Garvey and

The Waid Hill mausoleum is the only one made of brick and was one of the first lots sold at Oakland. Note the well-kept plot to the left, which is owned and maintained by Peter and Annette Mayfield. *Photo by Robert Gaare.*

Wooten appeared on the scene and tried to force the door open, but it was heavily bolted. One of the officers stood on a chair to look through the transom and saw what appeared to be a foot and bloodstains on the bed. Mrs. Johnson produced some keys that unlocked the door, and the gruesome sight was revealed.

Tony lay flat on his back, fully dressed, hat still on his head, his face smeared with blood. Bob lay on his back nearby, blood trickling from his right ear, one foot on the floor and one on the edge of the bed. Near his right hand was a large .36-caliber self-acting pistol, still smoking. The whole room smelled of burned gunpowder. Tony was already dead, but Bob still appeared to be breathing. Drs. Westmoreland and Avery arrived and lifted Bob to the bed. He let out a last sigh or groan and then expired.

Upon examination, the pistol was found to be a five-chambered weapon that was empty. There was the appearance of a scuffle from torn clothing about Tony's throat and bruises over Bob's left eye. The doctors believed that Bob shot Tony and then killed himself. An inquiry was held, and the jury concluded that the brothers were both under the influence. There had been a quarrel between the two of them, then one of them got the pistol out of the bookcase where it was kept and a tussle ensued. Bob fired the shots that killed his brother, and when he saw his brother was dead, he shot himself in the left temple. It was a fratricide/suicide and the case was closed.

The parents of the boys arrived from their home in Dallas, Georgia, late in the afternoon of the day of the shooting. Colonel D.P. Hill buried his face in his hands; the blow was terrible to him, as these boys were his only children.

Many people came to their funeral. The two were buried in unmarked graves beside the mausoleum of family patriarch Waid Hill. This is a very simple mausoleum and the only one at Oakland made of brick. The lot was one of the first lots sold at the cemetery. The mausoleum has since been completely bricked up as if the family wants to rest in peace with this tragedy.

Lewis Redwine: Bank Scandal

The period of time from January 24 to February 25, 1893, was known as "Black Week" in Atlanta, because it set a record for the most sensational crimes in any one month in Atlanta's history. Along with scandalous murders, attempted murders and suicides came the news that the doors of the Gate City National Bank were permanently closed due to default caused by the fraudulent actions of assistant cashier Lewis Redwine.

Lewis was a thirty-two-year-old bachelor and son of the noted Atlanta physician and druggist Dr. Columbus L. Redwine. As a bank employee, Lewis received a yearly salary of $1,500 but lived well beyond his means. He mingled in the best circles, lived at the posh Kimball House, was a member of the Capitol City Club, dressed well and entertained at lavish dinner and theatre parties. He had been embezzling money from the bank for quite some time, but he always managed to keep his accounts "fixed for the count."

By February 22, Lewis began to realize he was being suspected of bank theft. On that day, he was summoned to Bank President L.J. Hill's office. Instead he went to Buckalew's Saloon on the ground floor, had a stiff drink and fled. There was an intensive manhunt for him, along with a $1,000 reward. By then news of the bank's default was widespread. Everyone who had money and lost it in the Gate City Bank wanted to find Lewis Redwine. On February 24, he was found at a boardinghouse where he was going by the name Mr. Lester.

Redwine was never able to account for all the money. In his indictment, Redwine implicated Tom Cobb Jackson, saying he got most of the money. Jackson was the twenty-four-year-old son of Captain Harry Jackson, an esteemed lawyer and prominent Atlantan who rose to his son's defense. He admitted his son too had a "mania for spending money" and that it had crossed his mind that his son might be involved. Adding fuel to the fire, young, despondent Tom (first husband of the beautiful Sarah Grant Jackson, who would later marry Governor John Marshall Slaton of Leo Frank trial fame) committed suicide while sitting in a carriage in front of his father's house on the day the Lewis Redwine scandal broke.

Now Tom Cobb Jackson could not speak in his own behalf. Captain Jackson, in his own immense grief, believing he was innocent, strove to clear his son's name. Of the $100,000 in missing bank monies, only a small amount was accounted for, the rest more than likely being checks that were torn up. No incriminating evidence was ever tied to his son. Captain Jackson wrote, "At times when I realize the extent of the infamy he [Redwine]has attempted to place on my dead son, I feel that no punishment would be too great...I am only doing for poor Cobb what he would have bravely done for me. There is ample vindication today when this desperate man gravely crosses the thresholds of the penitentiary."

The headlines of the Atlanta paper read, "He has gone, but the people of Atlanta are yet talking about him." At the jail where Redwine remained for a year, a family friend gave him a cot so he could be more comfortable. The anonymous friend did this to honor Lewis's father, who had given him over $200 worth of medicine at a time when his family was sick and had no money. He wanted to repay the kindness by doing something nice for Dr. Redwine's troubled boy.

After release from the penitentiary, Lewis went to Texas and to Bowie, Louisiana, where strangely enough he worked as a bookkeeper for a lumber business. He died in 1900 at only forty-two and is buried in an unmarked grave at Oakland. His mother has a tall angel memorial erected on the family plot in her honor. It stands across from the grandest of all Oakland mausoleums—the Austell.

As for the money the good banking citizens of Gate City Bank lost—the officers and directors (L.J. Hill, A.W. Hill and E.S. Candless) made good the money lost because of the crime of a bank employee. Most of the payback came out of their own pockets.

CHAPTER 5

Politicians and Judges

There is a history in all men's lives.
−William Shakespeare, King Henry IV

LOGAN EDWIN BLECKLEY

Described as "this long limbed, large-brained son of the mountains," Judge Logan Edwin Bleckley was regarded by the legal fraternity as one of the greatest lawyers ever born in the state of Georgia.

Born in Rabun County on a Blue Ridge hilltop, Bleckley's sole garment through childhood was a cotton flannel gown, which he ditched at age twelve when he got his first pair of shoes. His father was clerk of court for the Superior, Inferior and Ordinary Courts in Rabun County. Young Bleckley would help copy his father's law papers, which gave him an early love for the law. He would borrow a lawbook from a traveling circuit lawyer, read it for six months, give it back to that lawyer the next time he came to town and borrow another one. The lawyers humored him, but later on when he started discussing learned questions raised in these books with precocious intelligence, they were astounded.

At nineteen he was admitted to the Georgia bar and started practicing in Rabun County, due to the "absence of money," as he called it. Earning only forty-five dollars in his first year of practice, he realized there was to be no gold mine for him in Rabun County and he set his sights for Atlanta. He traveled with little money for six days and nights, hoping the good people on his way would put him up. On the sixth day he began to wonder if he'd ever get out of the mountains. He was following the Western and Atlantic Railroad track. He had never seen a train before and when he arrived in a little village he thought with certainty that finally this must be Atlanta—it was Dalton. Logan was traveling westward, following the railroad and was as far from Atlanta as he had been on day one. He felt so foolish that he didn't know south from west, being without a compass, and he sold his horse and saddlebags, buying a train ticket to Atlanta. He called himself a "blamed ignoramus" and ended up working for the railroad for two years.

Then he set his sights on being elected the solicitor general of the Coweta circuit, which included Atlanta, as he believed it to be the best paying job in the state. He competed against nine other men, but he was the one elected. Eventually he went into private law practice with Basil H. Overby, known as the best practitioner, and John Brown Gordon, known as the best orator. Bleckley was known as the best legal mind. The three partners married daughters of General Hugh Harralson of La Grange, Overby marrying the oldest daughter, Elizabeth; Gordon the youngest daughter, Fanny; and Bleckley the middle daughter, Clara Caroline. Bleckley called his marriage to her the "crowning success of his whole life."

When the Civil War came, Bleckley enlisted in the Confederate army, undergoing training at "a camp of instruction, endeavoring to acquire some skill in the mobile art of homicide." A pacifist by nature—"I loved my friends but I did not hate my enemies"—fortunately he was never forced to commit homicide. He was honorably discharged for health reasons and then became a legal advisor to the state of Georgia, a reporter for the state supreme court, associate justice and eventually chief justice.

His court decisions were made not with ease and facility, but instead with pain and travail. "I reconsider, revise, scrutinize, revise the scrutiny, and scrutinize the revision…the law is too often unknown." But he was well known for his reports, opinions and his brilliant legal mind that allowed him "to make plain that which was confused and to make simple that which was difficult."

Some examples of his rulings follow:

Roberts v. Tift, Sixtieth Georgia: "The true law everywhere and at all times delighteth in the payment of just debts…the best possible thing to be done with a debt is to pay it."

Crumbly v. State, Sixty-first Georgia: "Fun is rather energetic even for Christmas times when it looks like a disposition to indulge in a little free and easy homicide. Shooting powder guns at a man as a practical joke is among the forbidden sports."

Marshal v. State, Fifty-ninth Georgia: "To be too drunk to form the intent to kill, he must have been too drunk to form the intent to shoot."

Bleckley was over six feet tall, lanky, loose jointed and of ill health most of his life, although he lived to be eighty years old. People said "he made little acquaintance with the barber's scissors" and liked being compared to Moses in his appearance. Once he appeared at a dinner of his old friend Dr. Miller dressed like so: "My beaver hat and Prince Albert coat are for any professional men I might meet. These brogan shoes are worn for comfort and in deference to any laboring man or farmer who might be present; these overalls are for the mechanics; and as I suspected I might chance to encounter a 'dude' or two, I wore this blue cravat and brought along this sporting walking stick."

When he retired to the mountains, to his veritable paradise, he took it upon himself to go to college, since his own education had been a self-taught one. His home in Clarksville was near the home of University of Georgia Chancellor Walter B. Hill. At the age of seventy-three, Bleckley wanted to study mathematics, "the reading of the root," a problem he wrestled with until his death. He proposed a four-day course of study to Chancellor Hill, who thought it was a good joke. But when Logan wrote to Hill, "I'm on my way to college," he realized differently. Logan set the all-time record for "educational sprinting," passing through his freshman, sophomore, junior and senior years in four days' time, one day for each grade level. At the end of the fourth day, he declared himself graduated.

When Bleckley retired from his second stint as chief justice, he wrote this oft-quoted poem:

> *Rest for hand and brow and breast,*
> *For fingers, heart and brain!*
> *Rest and peace! A long release*
> *From labor and from pain;*
> *Pain of doubt, fatigue, despair,*
> *Pain of darkness everywhere,*
> *And seeking light in vain.*
> *Peace and rest! Are they the best*
> *For mortals here below?*
> *Is soft repose from work and woes*
> *A bliss for men to know?*
> *Bliss of time is bliss of toil!*
> *No bliss but this from sun and soil*
> *Does God permit to grow.*

His admirers said that last stanza "should be burned into the heart of every young man. This is the essence of common sense, the conclusion of the human experience, the ultimate dogma of religion."

Logan Edwin Bleckley lies in soft repose in a simple, mounded grave at Oakland, nothing but a plain marker to mark the greatness of the man.

A simple stone mound marks the grave of colorful Judge Logan Edwin Bleckley, honoring his mountain roots. Bell Tower Ridge. *Photo by Robert Gaare.*

THE BROWNS: JOSEPH EMERSON, ELIZABETH GRISHAM AND JOSEPH MACKEY

The Browns were known as Georgia's "father and son combo who spanned a century of Georgia's political history."

Beginning with the father, Joseph Emerson Brown will forever be known, in spite of all his other accomplishments, as Georgia's Civil War governor. But he was also one of the state's most noted sons. Coming from humble beginnings, a young mountaineer (similar to Logan Bleckley's start), he traveled with a yoke of oxen to the Calhoun Academy in South Carolina to trade for room and board. He went to school there on credit. Then he worked his way down to Canton, Georgia, to open an academy, becoming a successful teacher who believed, "Toll is the sire of fame." He lived what he preached. Teaching himself law, he was admitted to the bar in 1845, entering politics as a state senator from Cherokee and Cobb Counties. He emerged as the leader of the Democrats. It was the beginning of a new regime. "Joe" Brown is what people loved to call him, a man of humble beginnings and a man of the people.

The Brown obelisk honoring Civil War Governor Joseph Emerson Brown, his wife Elizabeth and son Joseph Mackey Brown. Knit Mill section. *Photo by Robert Gaare.*

He became a judge in the Blue Ridge circuit, and there are those who say he was the best judge they ever had. In 1857, he ran for governor against Benjamin Harvey Hill, the most popular orator ever in the state of Georgia. Joe, in contrast, talked in a simple style with a homegrown philosophy. This style hit home with Georgians, one of whom said, "I confess Mr. Hill is a great orator, but he lacks judgment and common sense." The ladies of Cherokee County made Joe Brown a calico quilt. It was said that wealthy Ben Hill wouldn't repose under one of those.

The newly elected Joe Brown was destined to butt heads with the prominent Georgians. Their disapproval affected him not at all. He was so popular a governor that in his second election he received more than double the majority of his first election and remained governor for an unprecedented four terms. But he will always be remembered as Georgia's Civil War governor. During the war, the generals wanted him to stay. The political elite agreed and deemed it unwise to elect someone new in the midst of wartime. He was a model war governor and was called "a veritable Stonewall Jackson among the state executives."

When the war was over, Governor Brown continued to go about the business of the state until the governor's mansion was surrounded by Federal soldiers. He was told he had thirty minutes to make his departure arrangements and was then hurried to Washington and incarcerated in the Old Capitol Prison. He soon had a meeting with President Andrew Johnson, during which he agreed to support the abolition of slavery, accept the end of the Confederacy, support Andrew Johnson's administration and accept amnesty between North and South. Then he was released by executive order. However, he was not allowed to resume his gubernatorial duties, as Georgia was under military rule. According to acting military commander General James H. Wilson, "The restoration of peace and order could not be entrusted to rebels and traitors who destroyed the peace and trampled down the order that had existed more than half a century in Georgia."

Brown became a Republican and in so doing many saw him as a turncoat. He aligned himself with the carpetbag government of Georgia in order to hasten Reconstruction in the state. "To be governed without representation is ludicrous," was his reasoning. In an 1880 speech to the General Assembly he said, "I feel I have been true to you, my state, my country. I told you the truth when it was exceedingly unpalatable."

The state government was twice destroyed and twice rebuilt during the Reconstruction period of 1865–77. Not until the new constitution was approved in 1877 was the power restored to the people of Georgia. This constitution remains in effect today.

When he died, Joe Brown was said to be worth $12 million; this man who came from simple means became one of the richest and most powerful men in Georgia. A statue of Governor Joseph Emerson Brown and his wife, Elizabeth Grisham Brown, stands on the state capitol grounds. Elizabeth is seated, with her husband standing by her side, his hand on her shoulder. Her inclusion marks the only statue of a woman (other than Georgia's Lady Liberty on top of the capitol dome) on the grounds.

Their son, Joseph Mackey Brown, was forever known as "Little Joe Brown" and was honored in this song by Julia Spalding:

> *In this fine old state of Georgia, not so many years ago,*
> *Lived a patriot of the people by the simple name of Joe.*
> *But he made that name immortal, you remember Joe E. Brown?*
> *And he left a son that's like him, Little Joe they'll write him down.*

A graduate of Oglethorpe University with the highest scholastic average in his class, Little Joe was admitted to the bar in Canton, Georgia, in 1873. He developed an eye condition that handicapped him for the rest of his life, preventing him from doing the massive amount of reading and writing required of a lawyer. He went to work for the Western and Atlantic Railroad as the traffic manager. A tiff he had with then-Governor Hoke Smith over the lowering of passenger fares (Joe was not in favor of this) marked the beginning of their epic political duel.

In the gubernatorial election of 1908, Little Joe Brown challenged Hoke Smith. He made no campaign speeches and gave only fifteen statements for newspaper publication. The largest number of voters in Georgia history turned out to vote, and Little Joe won by a landslide. His victory resulted largely from the anti-Smith backwash. Smith was a very unpopular governor over policies that resulted in economic hardships for many Georgians. A campaign slogan like "Hoke and Hunger, Brown and Bread," was all it took to put Little Joe in the governor's mansion. Julia Spalding's song of 1908 also helped. The first verse was printed earlier; the second follows below:

> *He's a chip of the same old block; His word is round as a rock.*
> *Oh he's not a bit like Hoke, who will blow away in smoke,*
> *In a very little while and that's no joke.*
> *It's no use to run him down, he'll get the votes in every town.*
> *Hurray, boys, for Little Joe Brown.*

His adversarial relationship with Hoke continued throughout his two-year term, at the end of which he again found himself in a race against

The marble relief of Elizabeth Grisham Brown, Georgia's first lady during the Civil War. *Photo by Robert Gaare.*

Hoke, who had regained his popularity. Hoke won round two. But when a U.S. Senate seat opened up in Georgia, Hoke resigned from his governor's job to go to Washington as one of Georgia's senators. John Slaton filled the governor's seat for the rest of that term. Little Joe ran in 1912, without Hoke as an opponent, and easily won. He challenged Hoke for the Senate seat in 1914, and even though it was his "turn" to win, Little Joe lost and never returned to the political arena. The two adversaries buried their personal differences in 1928 when they both supported Al Smith for the presidency. Little Joe was too ill to campaign, but was photographed with his former rival at Al Smith's headquarters.

Father, son and mother Brown are buried under an elaborate memorial in a prominent location at Oakland. Mother Elizabeth comes across as the star of the family, her busted silhouette gorgeously carved into her monument, which stands front and center on the plot.

Hoke Smith is also buried at Oakland, but in a diagonally opposite corner of the cemetery.

BENJAMIN HARVEY HILL

Born in 1823 to a moneyed, Georgia plantation family, Benjamin Harvey Hill was ever the elegant, eloquent statesman and in many ways the opposite of the Browns.

Hill, along with his wife and children, nestled into their plantation Bellevue in LaGrange. The mansion has been restored and is available in all its antebellum elegance for tours and viewings.

Hill was the opponent to Joseph Emerson Brown in the gubernatorial election of 1857. Man of the people, Joe Brown won the election. When the Civil War was imminent and the state of Georgia was to vote on whether or not to join South Carolina in the Confederacy, Benjamin Harvey Hill, a strong Union man, wanted to vote no. But when the state's fate was sealed with the Confederacy, he saw that he had no other choice than to go with the majority. Ironically, he became one of Jefferson Davis's strongest supporters, serving in the Confederate Senate. When asked who he considered to be his staunchest ally, Jefferson Davis answered unflinchingly: Benjamin Harvey Hill.

During the final months of the war, when Federal forces under Colonel Oscar LaGrange overtook Hill's hometown of LaGrange, Bellevue was strangely spared. Colonel LaGrange (just a coincidence that his name is the same as the town's) had a soft spot for Benjamin Harvey Hill. A niece of Hill's had tended to the colonel when he was seriously wounded and captured by the Confederates in the spring of 1864. He recovered and was eventually exchanged for Southern prisoners that fall. But he never forgot this favor, and he spared the Hill home in return. The Hills had another home in Athens, Georgia, which also escaped the Yankee torches and serves today as the home for the president of the University of Georgia.

During the Reconstruction period in Georgia, Hill made stirring pro-South speeches, denouncing any and all efforts by the Federal military occupation of Georgia to further humiliate the South. He conceded in 1870 and joined forces with Joe Brown to work out the conciliation with the provisional government in order to bring a quicker end to the Reconstruction and military rule in Georgia. He too was strongly criticized for being a turncoat, but bounced back in popularity to represent Georgia in the U.S. Senate in 1877. He was well known on the national scene for his great eloquence as a stirring orator. Tragically, he died of cancer, which affected his eloquent tongue and stirring speech and silenced him at the young age of fifty-eight.

Several years after Hill's death, a monument in downtown Atlanta was erected in his honor. Crowds filled the streets to an astounding capacity, which perhaps had something to do with Jefferson Davis's arrival to view the unveiling. A local newspaper editor wrote, "Everybody in DeKalb, who can, will go to Atlanta next Saturday to see Jeff Davis one more time before the Grand Old Man passes from earth to heaven. We hope on that day to hear the real, old fashioned rebel yell. We reckon it will offend no one, but if so, let it offend." The next time Jefferson Davis came to town was in his funeral cortege.

On the day Hill's monument was unveiled, the crowds were dense with Confederate war veterans who watched children strew flowers in the pathway to the speakers' platform. There was much pomp and circumstance that day, as much to honor the short glory days of the Confederacy as to honor Benjamin Harvey Hill. Everyone held their breath as General Longstreet made a surprise appearance. As he walked toward Jefferson Davis, everyone wondered what would happen, as the two men had been at odds since the war ended. Thunderous applause erupted as the two men embraced. Grand speeches were made by General Clement Anselm Evans (buried at Oakland), Henry Grady (temporarily interred at Oakland) and Jefferson Davis himself. The statue that stands in the center of Atlanta was then unveiled.

Hill and his wife Caroline Holt Hill reside at Oakland, close to Hoke Smith's plot, on the southeastern edges. On his tall marble shaft the inscription reads:

Benjamin H. Hill, when too feeble to speak wrote the following:
"If a grain of corn will die and
Then rise again in so much beauty,
Why may I not die, and then rise
Again in infinite beauty and life?
How is the last a greater mystery
Than the first? And by as much as I
Exceed the grain of corn in
This life, why may not I exceed it
In the new life?
How can we limit the power of
Him who made the grain of corn
And then made the same grain arise
In such wonderful newness of life!"

CHAPTER 6

The Confederate Section

Let us in this grand land of ours, rebuild each waste, restore each barren spot, improve her, forward her, until she blossoms like a rose, amongst nations at the feet of our heroes; and tell them this we learned from you; this we did for you.
—From Colonel Albert H. Cox's Confederate Memorial Day speech at Oakland Cemetery, 1887

ATLANTA LADIES MEMORIAL ASSOCIATION

It is fitting to begin this section with the women's organization that made it all possible. The oldest patriotic organization in our country is the Atlanta Ladies Memorial Association (AMLA), formed in 1866, one year after the end of the Civil War. The organization petitioned the city council for donation of ground in Oakland Cemetery for the purpose of interring Confederate veterans and other war dead. With the permission and land, the ladies got to work.

Members and their husbands spent the fall of 1867 raising the necessary funds to pay for the arduous task of removing bodies that had been hastily buried in shallow trenches from battles fought in or near Atlanta during the spring and summer of 1864. It was their goal to give each "neglected hero" a Christian burial and a grave in the Confederate section of Oakland. Wood was donated for the coffins and markers. Then the gruesome search began.

As many as ninety bodies were found in some of the trenches. The soldiers had been wrapped in their blankets, faces up, hands crossed over their chests and kepi hats covering their faces. When the bodies were exposed to the air, many of them crumbled to dust. Whatever was left was lovingly gathered and placed in coffins. It cost two dollars apiece to remove the bodies and provide the coffin or box for the remains of the three thousand or so unknown soldiers they interred.

The Confederate Obelisk, surrounded by graves of Confederate soldiers. At one time this was the tallest structure in Atlanta. *Photo by Eric Gaare.*

The first president of the organization was Mrs. Joseph Morgan (Eugenia Hamilton Goode), who with her husband and the Claytons (Mrs. W.W. Clayton and daughters Julia and Sallie) cleaned the cemetery and raised the necessary funds to make new markers. Colonel Joseph Morgan personally painted the headstones that replaced the markers of the identified soldiers, whose identities were marked in pencil on rotten pieces of plank. Most of the deaths of these identified soldiers occurred from 1862 through 1864, many dying in the local Atlanta military hospitals. Procuring the Book of the Dead required the opening of a vault in the state capitol in Milledgeville. Mrs. John C. Milledge (Fannie) secured it and copied it from the records. Green A. Pilgrim was the sexton of Oakland Cemetery during the Civil War but left during the Federal occupation. No deaths or burials were recorded during this time period, late summer and fall of 1864, as the book had been taken to Milledgeville for safekeeping.

Some 1,000 headstones were redone in this first project by the Ladies Memorial Association. There were 4,348 known graves and 3,000 unknown, totaling almost 7,500 graves at Oakland for Confederate soldiers. At least 20 graves were of Federal soldiers who probably died in Atlanta Hospitals and were prisoners of war.

The Confederate Section

Dr. J.P. Logan, who was chief surgeon of Atlanta in 1863, said Confederate and Union soldiers were buried indiscriminately and intermixed, to his chagrin. "Brave men who have died for our cause were buried next to worthless invaders of our soil…we should not be guilty of neglect of our own." He apologized for not discovering this oversight sooner and tried to prevent the placing of any more enemies amongst the Confederate honored dead. These twenty remain, their markers originally painted blue.

Due to Atlanta's active termite population, the wooden markers so painstakingly painted in 1866 were replaced by stone markers in the late 1880s. These markers record the soldier's name (last and first initial), name of the company, number of the infantry and the state he came from. Iron crosses are on the Confederate graves. There are shields on the Union graves that resemble interstate symbols. The older ones are rounded and the newer ones are pointed.

Mrs. Mary Williams of Columbus, Georgia, is credited with starting the first Confederate Memorial Day in Georgia to honor the soldiers by embellishing their graves with flowers and flags. She proposed April 26, the day Confederate Joseph Johnston surrendered to Federal General William T. Sherman. She vowed that great eulogies and speeches would be given on this day to "pay honor to those who died defending the life, honor, and happiness of the Southern women." One of those men to be honored was her own husband, Colonel C.J. Williams, who died from disease contracted in camp during the first Virginia campaign. Georgia was the first state to declare Confederate Memorial Day a legal holiday, celebrating the first Confederate Memorial Day on April 26, 1866.

It wasn't long before the Ladies Memorial Association embarked on another Oakland project. The Milledges, the Morgans and some one hundred other members wanted a Confederate Memorial monument built to serve as the focal point for the Confederate section. The granite for the monument was donated by the Venables, who owned Stone Mountain. They laid the cornerstone on the date of Robert E. Lee's burial, October 12, 1870. Into the cornerstone they sealed a likeness of General Lee, two miniature Confederate flags, Confederate money and stamps, the names on the roster of the Ladies Memorial Association, a bullet that killed a Confederate soldier, a white glove belonging to a Mason and a lady's kid glove. All of these items were wrapped in an 1862 Confederate flag and set in stone.

The memorial was completed in 1874 and was unveiled on Confederate Memorial Day. At sixty-five feet high, the obelisk stands three stories and was the tallest structure in Atlanta for many years. The ceremony started at noon and lasted for half a day with parades, speeches, bands and the placing of flags, wreaths and flowers on the graves. Colonel George T. Fry gave the speech that day. Parts are quoted below:

> *While we tenderly cherish the memorial of the dead, let us also with kindness and sympathy remember the worthy living. This memorial was erected by loving hearts and tender hands to the memory of our Confederate dead…Let us renew our vows of fidelity to the memory of the brave, and to the flag of our common country, the Constitution, and the Union…as a people we know the horrors of war and the value of peace. We know that our government is greater, grander, freer, and better than any other on earth. This knowledge is worth the price it cost us.*

Captain Ellis also spoke: "We make no apologies for worshipping at the shrine of our dead heroes…Teach your children who these dead men were. Tell them of their lofty courage; instruct them in their virtues." Then there was a procession of war veterans, described in the Atlanta paper as "battle scarred veterans who had come to pay tribute to their fallen comrades."

The ladies continued with one final project. In 1891, they deeded some of their property to the Hebrew congregation for $2,000 and used that money to start the design work on the Lion of Lucerne. (See the next section for details.)

Fannie Milledge continued her work with the association as president for fourteen years until her death on April 25, 1895, one day short of the thirtieth anniversary of Johnston's surrender. She and her husband are buried close to the grave of General John B. Gordon and his wife, Fanny. Eugenia Morgan remained active until her death in 1924. She and her husband Joseph are also buried in the Confederate section.

The organization was dying out, literally. All of the original members had passed on by the early 1900s. Time and apathy caused the organization to shrink in numbers and the Memorial Day crowds to shrink with them. In 1973, a marker was dedicated at Oakland to honor the first daughters of the Confederacy and the work done by the original members of the Atlanta Ladies Memorial Association.

Although the crowds today are small on Confederate Memorial Days and the number of flags placed are fewer, the speeches are still thought provoking and stirring. One recent speech given by Dr. Judson C. Ward Jr., eminent historian and dean of faculties at Emory, rang out with these words:

> *The southern soldier saw his cause as defending his land from invasion, his home from devastation. The dead buried here are also Americans. This was a brothers' war in which the nation lost potential poets, painters,*

inventors, and statesmen on both sides. This is not a day for stirring up sectional strife, but a day to be proud of, a day to honor those who did their duty as they saw it…It is a part of our history, a part of our heritage.

SWITZERLAND'S LION OF LUCERNE

Mark Twain called it the "saddest and most moving piece of rock in the world"—the dying lion that is carved into the side of a sandstone cliff in Lucerne, Switzerland. The lion commemorated the heroic defeat and final fight of the loyal Swiss guards who were protecting French King Louis XVI and his wife, Marie Antoinette. It was 1792 when the king and queen were whisked to safety at their palace at Tuileries in Paris. On August 10, working-class Parisians stormed the palace, trying to get to their hated king and queen, who lived in the grandest of styles. The Swiss regiment of the Royal Guards were under order by the king to lay down their arms. He did not know this action would result in their massacre. More than seven hundred Swiss officers died that day without knowing the king and queen had fled the palace.

The Swiss, though politically neutral, have a long history of supplying mercenaries to foreign governments and are well known for honoring their agreements, even unto death. Danish artist Bertel Thorvaldsen carved the lion in 1821 into a sandstone cliff above the center of Lucerne near the Glacier Garden. The dying lion is carved with his paw over the shield bearing the French fleur-de-lis of the Bourbon King Louis XVI. The broken lance pierces his loyal heart. Into the rock is carved "The Loyalty and Bravery of the Swiss," along with the names of those who sacrificed their lives that day.

ATLANTA'S LION OF THE CONFEDERACY

Georgia's version of the Lion of Lucerne was carved in 1894 out of the largest piece of marble quarried from Georgia up to that time. The sculptor was T.M. Brady of Canton, Georgia, who received much admiration for his work. With a few exceptions, it is a near copy of the Swiss version. Atlanta's lion guards a field containing the remains of three thousand unknown Confederate soldiers who died in the Atlanta campaign. Under the lion lie boxes containing amputated limbs of soldiers. Georgia's version was unveiled on April 26, 1894, Confederate Memorial Day, and twenty years after the unveiling of the Confederate obelisk.

The Lion of the Confederacy, guarding the three thousand graves of the unknown Confederate soldiers, mostly from the Atlanta campaign. Lion Square. *Photo by Eric Gaare.*

Flowers had to be shipped from Brunswick, Georgia, as a late frost had killed all the local ones. Four companies of men led the procession to the statue. The Honorable H.H. Carlton from Athens gave the speech.

Over the years many differing interpretations have arisen as to the symbolism and meaning of the statue. Most say that the lion is a symbol of a noble and innocent creature, suffering from the pain of his own mortal wounds. Some say he is suffering from the inconsolable grief of losing his master, and he must bear his sufferings alone. Forever silent, we still hear the depth of his anguish. He rests on the Confederate flag with a spear in his back to represent courage in death. The tears on his face are in remembrance of the just, though defeated, cause. Some say his jaws are bared in defiance. Some say he represents a young soldier struck down at the height of his career. Some say he represents an early death before reaching full potential. He lies with the flag as his pillow and comforter with his scabbard and sword lying beside him. He guards the dust of the unknown Confederate dead and moves all who come to see him.

The Oakland Magnolia

Stretching out over the lion of Atlanta was Oakland's largest magnolia tree, with branches spreading out over sixty feet, sheltering the lion and the graves of the unknown. It was said to have been one of the finest specimen of magnolia trees in all of Georgia. But it is no more.

In 1998, the tree fell to disease and was removed on December 3. Renowned *Atlanta Journal-Constitution* reporter Celestine Sibley wrote a touching article about the tree's importance. Regretfully, she could not attend the burial ceremony for the tree. But for those who did, it was reported there was not a dry eye at the site. The Alfred Holt Colquitt Chapter of the United Daughters of the Confederacy and Historic Oakland Foundation placed a commemorative marker where the tree once stood. It reads:

> *"To everything there is a season, and a time to every purpose under the heaven: A time to be born, and a time to die; a time to plant, and a time to pluck up that which is planted." Ecclesiastes 3:1–2*
> *Over 100 years old, origin unknown, but duty well done. Guardian of the Unknown Confederate Dead, sheltering arms for Atlanta's beloved Lion. Never to be forgotten, but living through those left behind. December 3, 1998*

A few saplings have emerged. The great magnolia shall rise again.

Fuller/Caine/Murphy: The Great Locomotive Chase

This is one action and adventure story that never gets old. On April 12, 1862, twenty Federal soldiers from Ohio posed as Kentuckians on their way to enlist in a Southern regiment. Instead these men, forever known as Andrews Raiders, stole the locomotive named the *General*, its tender and three boxcars at Big Shanty (now known as Kennesaw, Georgia). Their intent was to cut supply lines to Atlanta by burning up bridges and tearing up rails all the way into Tennessee. They managed to travel ninety miles northward before they were captured by Captain William Fuller, Jefferson Caine and Anthony Murphy.

It took three locomotives—the *Texas*, the *Yonah* and the *William K. Smith*—to catch up to the *General*, just south of the Georgia and Tennessee border. The honors for the capture went to Captain Fuller and the *Texas*, which

Six Feet Under, a great bar and restaurant across the street from Oakland, seen peeking through the Egyptian-style Kontz memorial. *Photo by Eric Gaare.*

caught the *General* from behind. This chase was to go down in history as one of the greatest exploits of the Civil War.

Captain Andrews and seven of his men were caught on foot as they tried to escape into the woods. Andrews was publicly executed as a spy somewhere in downtown Atlanta. The seven men captured with him were hanged on the fringes of Oakland Cemetery on June 18, 1862. Captain Green J. Foreacre, in his newly appointed job as Atlanta's provost marshal, handled the execution. A marker at Oakland designates the spot where they were hanged, which is today within view of the Six Feet Under Restaurant on Memorial Drive.

As for the rest of the raiders, eight escaped from the Fulton County jail to make it back to the Federal lines. Six were later exchanged as prisoners of war. Two of the Federal soldiers overslept that morning and missed the entire adventure. The executed Federal soldiers were eventually taken to the National Cemetery in Chattanooga for permanent interment. Captain Andrews has a special tribute on his grave. It reads, "Ohio's tribute to the Andrews Raiders, 1862." It was erected in 1890 and has a bronzed miniature of the *General* on top. The Federal government posthumously awarded the Raiders the first official Congressional Medals of Honor.

The three heroes of the day for the Confederacy—Captain William Fuller, Anthony Murphy and Jefferson Caine—are all buried at Oakland. Captain Fuller's grave has an obelisk with the story of his part in the recapturing of the *General* inscribed on the sides. It's difficult to read now due to the weathering, but says in part, "On April 2, 1862, Cpt. Fuller pursued and after a race of 90 miles from Big Shanty northward on the Western and Atlantic Railroad, recaptured the historic war-engine 'General' which had been seized by 22 Federal soldiers in disguise, thereby preventing destruction of the bridges of the railroad and the consequent dismemberment of the Confederacy."

Hangman Green J. Foreacre is also buried at Oakland.

The *General* resides in all its glory in Kennesaw, Georgia, at the Southern Civil War Museum, where the story is told daily to tourists and schoolchildren. The *Texas* abides at the Cyclorama in Atlanta's Grant Park.

There's a bit more to tell so read on…

CONDUCTOR JAMES BELL: THE STORY OF THE *GENERAL* CONTINUES

James Bell knew the train the *General* from childhood and because he knew her so well, he supervised her restoration in as authentic a manner as possible. In his youth, he had served as oiler and wiper of the famous engine. An engineer himself for most of his adulthood, he had a vast knowledge of locomotives from Georgia. He knew that the *Georgia*, a Norris engine (meaning a kettle-domed hook motion locomotive), had blown up in Calhoun, Georgia, in 1862; the *Swiftsure*, a Rogers engine (meaning a double-domed link motion locomotive), was splintered by a shell from Sherman's siege guns; and he knew the story of the *General* and how it was dismantled on that wild, adventurous day. He also knew that the miniature bronze locomotive placed on a granite pedestal at the Chattanooga gravesite of James Andrews and the Seven Raiders was patterned after a coal-burning engine that was used to haul freight and cattle back then and is a laughable interpretation of the real thing. So yes, he was the man for the job of restoring the *General*.

During the Civil War, Bell's job was to supervise the transportation of Confederate troops between Atlanta and Montgomery. He longed for action, so he secured a transfer to join in the fight. And then he made history. Sergeant James Bell of the Seventh Georgia Regiment was fighting the enemy near Fair Oaks, Virginia, in October of 1864. Late in the day, his regiment became separated from the other Confederate commands and was trying to hold a position behind breastworks near an overgrown field. There was a lull in the fighting and it appeared the Federal soldiers had pulled back. His regiment took a much needed rest, but not Bell. He climbed the breastworks and crossed the weedy field to a ravine, where he stopped suddenly in shock. There lay the entire Federal regiment, and there he was, the lone soldier in gray. Realizing his plight, he concocted a daredevil scheme of all or nothing, fired his musket and shouted, "Surrender! Lay down your arms!" The bewildered Yankees believed the enemy was in full force behind Bell and they'd been caught with their pants down. They rose up one after the other and surrendered their weapons to the solitary Bell. His regiment, having heard the shouts and gunfire, quickly followed their ears and found Sergeant James L. Bell holding three hundred captured Yankees from the Nineteenth Wisconsin Regiment.

This surrender was hailed as the most wonderful achievement in the history of warfare and would never be equaled. The captured Yankees, no doubt extremely embarrassed, were sent to Richmond as prisoners of war. The captured flag of the Nineteenth Wisconsin is on view at the Georgia capitol with an inscription honoring Bell.

After the war, Bell wondered what became of the Wisconsin Regiment soldier in charge of that flag. He had been the last one to surrender. Bell placed an inquiry in the Wisconsin papers and was told the gentleman was John Fallen (no pun intended), and he died in 1881.

Much later on, when President Teddy Roosevelt visited Atlanta, he insisted Captain Bell visit him in his railroad touring car, where he conducted a long interview with Bell. When the train arrived in Tuskegee, Alabama, Roosevelt insisted Captain Bell stand beside him on the platform while he made a speech. Captain Bell, although a lifelong Democrat, had many positive things to say about the Republican Roosevelt.

Serving more than forty-five years with the West Point Railroad, Captain Bell was given a stripe to wear for every five years of service. That meant he wore a total of nine heavy stripes. It was reported that one sleeve was so heavy with gold that "only the stalwart military figure of Cpt. Bell keeps his uniform from hanging one-sided from his broad shoulders." He died on May 12, 1918, and is buried at Oakland.

THE COMMON CONFEDERATE SOLDIER

Amongst the rows and rows of markers and graves of fallen Confederate soldiers representing various states, companies, battalions and regiments, several catch your attention.

Side by side sit the markers of F.M. Croft and Mrs. Croft (no first name given). She is the only female known to be buried amongst the military graves. Her husband's marker reads, "FM CROFT, 5th Georgia, Company H, CSA, died April 18, 1864." Hers reads, "MRS. CROFT, wife of FM CROFT, GA INF, CSA, April 19, 1864." Their burials occurred one day

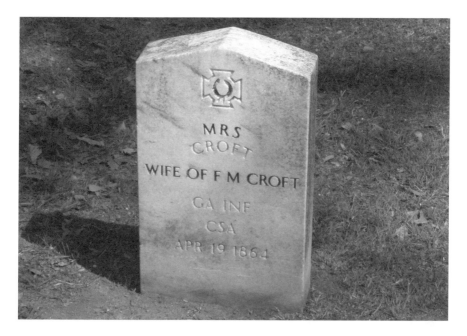

Mrs. Croft is the only known woman to be buried in the Confederate section. Her husband's marker is beside hers. *Photo by Eric Gaare.*

John Brown Gordon, the "Idol of Georgians," Civil War hero, U.S. senator and governor of Georgia. Generals' Corner. *Photo by Eric Gaare.*

apart. There is no more information on the two of them, leaving us to speculate: was she impersonating a male soldier in order to be near her husband? There were four hundred known women in the Civil War who did just that. Were Mr. and Mrs. Croft wounded together, perhaps in the Atlanta campaign, and she expired the day after he did? Did she commit suicide the day after she heard of her husband's death? Did she die of a broken heart? We can only imagine the true story.

Private Lucian B. Weakley, who died at Chickamauga, lies buried underneath a large sprawling magnolia tree, one of the most impressive in the cemetery. In 1885, his brother placed a sprout from a magnolia behind his brother's grave. It took root and now stands fully mature, over one hundred years old, keeping his brother's grave protected from the elements.

The Oakland Generals: Featuring John Brown Gordon

Five Confederate generals are buried at Oakland. John Brown Gordon, Clement Anselm Evans and Alfred Iverson Jr. are buried in Generals' Corner of the Confederate section. William Stephen Walker and Lucius Jeremiah Gartrell are buried in family plots.

John Brown Gordon, known as the "Idol of Georgians," entered the Civil War with no military training, but quickly distinguished himself on the battlefield. Possessing "splendid audacity," he was described by one Confederate officer as a "splendid picture of gallantry standing in his stirrups, bareheaded, hat in hand, arms extended, and voice like a trumpet exhorting his men to battle." He once said his erect posture in the saddle saved his life when a Yankee bullet tore through the back of his coat instead of his spine, which it certainly would have done if he had ridden slumped over the saddle.

At Sharpsburg/Antietam, Gordon was ordered to hold an area known as Sunken Road. He held it in spite of being shot five times and losing part of his face on the left side. He would have drowned in his own blood had not a sixth bullet put a hole in his hat, allowing the blood to flow out. After recovering from his wounds, he sported a deep scar on the left side of his face, causing one soldier to say of him, "not the prettiest thing you ever did see on a field of fight. It 'ud put fight into a whipped chicken just to look at him." No doubt this is why an always bearded Gordon was consistently photographed from the right side.

He was happily married to Rebecca "Fanny" Harralson (the youngest Harralson daughter, noted earlier in the chapter on Judge Logan Bleckley, law partner), who traveled with him during the Civil War and nursed him back to health after he received multiple wounds at Sharpsburg. Toward the end of the war, she gave birth and had to stay behind while the soldiers marched on. She found herself behind enemy lines, which didn't faze her, as she was made of similar stuff as her husband. At the third battle of Winchester, Virginia, the story goes that she rushed out onto the streets shouting to her husband's retreating troops to go back and face the enemy. He was horrified to find her on the streets, dodging balls and shells.

Gordon would eventually lead the Army of Northern Virginia during its last parade at Appomattox, sparing General Lee the humility of being the one to formally surrender the arms and colors to Federal General Joshua L. Chamberlain. In his memoirs, Chamberlain recalled the noble spirit of Gordon and the Confederate troops and their gallant and bittersweet surrender.

At war's end, Gordon was one of the most popular men in the South. By the end of the first decade after the war, he was one of the most well-known and respected Southerners in the United States. Representing Georgia in the U.S. Senate, he defended the South, attempting to negate Northern prejudice and misconceptions by saying, "No people in the history of the world have ever been so misunderstood, so misjudged, and so cruelly maligned as the people of the South." He labored to remove all Federal troops from the South, and when they finally left Louisiana and South Carolina, the Reconstruction period was over.

Part of the Bourbon Triumvirate of Georgia (with Alfred Colquitt and Joseph Emerson Brown), Gordon was one of the most conspicuous figures in Georgia politics, serving for two terms as governor and as senator. He was heralded by Henry Grady, the voice behind the New South movement. But his name was linked with controversies and implied scandals, his main accuser being Rebecca Latimer Felton, a constant thorn in his side. Still he remained the "Idol of Georgians." During his last years he wrote his gentle *Reminiscences of the Civil War* and gave lectures that vindicated the South as well as heralded a new spirit of nationalism for the entire country.

In 1903, Gordon, his faithful wife Fanny and their six children and their families traveled to their winter home near Miami for a restful Christmas. He became ill and died several days later. The family received a flood of telegrams, including one from President Theodore Roosevelt. The Atlanta Ladies Memorial Association offered Fanny an Oakland plot for her husband and later for herself in what would be "Generals' Corner," in the Confederate section. She accepted and accompanied the body of her husband for the long train trip from Florida to Atlanta. His body lay in state while Confederate veterans and many others paid their respects. One old veteran approached the casket and asked if he could remove his jacket and place it on the coffin. When he lifted it off and put the coat back on, he sobbed, "Now thousands couldn't buy it from me."

Fanny survived her husband by twenty-seven years, joining him in 1931. Their plot is beautifully landscaped and well cared for, overlooking the Confederate obelisk and close to Clement Evans's grave. The two generals were born within one year of each other and died seven years apart, brothers in a lost cause and brothers at Oakland.

The Diarists:
Carrie Berry and Sarah Huff

Atlanta had two young women who kept diaries during the shelling and Federal occupation of Atlanta: Sarah Huff and Carrie Berry (Crumley). Both are buried at Oakland. Although Carrie Berry's diary is the better known—the original is owned and displayed at the Atlanta History Center—Sarah Huff's is the more interesting. Carrie, at nine years old, was chosen by her father to be the family chronicler. She wrote faithfully every day, but many times her entries are short and repetitive and read like a dreaded school lesson or obligatory chore. Sarah, on the other hand, wrote hers as a memoir when she was much older. She was definitely the more gifted writer. At this writing, only the first few chapters of Sarah's diary are available for viewing online.

Sarah Huff's memoir is entitled *My 80 Years in Atlanta*, including her impressions as an eight-year-old when Sherman and company shelled Atlanta. Daughter of Jeremiah and Elizabeth Norton Huff, she described herself as "history-minded and a lover of adventure; few other Atlanta children were ever born at a time so opportune." She and her sister never married and lived in the family home on Huff Road, off Marietta Street and Howell Road, for their entire lives. She loved to talk and reminisce about the old days, had a home filled with Civil War memorabilia and still wore her black lace-up boots into the 1940s.

Sarah hoarded her personal papers until finally sharing them with the superintendent of Atlanta's public schools. She wanted to pass on the traditions of the Old South.

One of her most vivid recollections goes back to when she was five. An excited neighbor rushed over to tell her mother that shots had been fired at Fort Sumter. The two ladies cried as "if it meant something very serious had taken place." Years passed before Sarah understood what it meant. She also remembers her eighteen-year-old cousin and her father enlisting in Cobb's

Carrie Berry Crumley, ten-year-old diarist during the siege, evacuation, occupation and burning of Atlanta in 1864. Original six acres. *Photo by Eric Gaare.*

Legion, Company B. Her mother cut the cloth to make their uniforms to wear to the war. She was crying as she basted and fitted the clothes on her menfolk. Her family's mammy added, "Everybody would have to go to the war and probably get kilt," which made Sarah join the weeping women. Her father had his daguerreotype made before the war. She and her mother wept many times over "that earnest face and manly figure."

A neighbor put up a button factory, furnishing bone buttons for the soldiers' uniforms. Sarah described the process as "wonderful, watching those button cutters come down on the thinly sliced bones." It became the most extensive button factory in the South.

She described the nearby Dexter Niles house, where the "transfer" took place, meaning the transfer of command over the Southern forces from the wildly popular General Joseph E. Johnston to the wildly unpopular General John B. Hood. In her colorful manner and storytelling style, Sarah described the sweet music played by the bands on that brilliant moonlit night with the weeping soldiers feeling the despair over the discharge of their idolized commander. At midnight when the watchman's voice sang out, "Twelve o'clock and all's well," the bells rang out as if ringing the death knell of the Confederacy.

During the war, her mother became "the major general of the farm forces and the commander in chief of the home guards," which consisted of two sons, an orphan boy, a slave and his two sons and Sarah. As all women were forced out of necessity to become "captains of industry" in the struggle for their daily bread, so did Sarah's mother. Each family had to strive to be self-sufficient, something that was difficult without the menfolk around to help. Growing wheat was one matter; threshing it was another. Sarah's neighbors brought over their threshing machines to stay at the Huffs' because they were going off to war to try "to thrash the North."

On July 20, 1864, Sarah heard the storm break loose—the Battle of Peachtree Creek. Within one mile of where she stood, trees as big as a man's body were mowed down by exploding shells. Churches, schools and houses were demolished. Cannon reports sounded like thunder. The musketry sounded like hail on the roof. Her brother shouted, "If they turn their guns this way we will all be torn to pieces." Sarah's mother refused to leave their house, even though all the neighbors had gone, except for the button factory neighbor, George Edwards. He just ran up the British flag over his house and the Huff house too, to save it from burning. The fight lasted less than a day but "the havoc wrought by its fury continued to show for more than a quarter of a century."

The Huff family found themselves in the line of fire. Soldiers came and commanded them to leave immediately. It turned out to be only a skirmish and a false alarm, but this was only known in retrospect. They packed up to leave and hurried into Atlanta, where they stayed at Charlie Shearer's house until the siege ended. Sarah saw many wounded and dead soldiers carted into the city. Men were clinging to the sides of the hospital vans to fan away the swarming flies that hovered over the victims' wounds. Her twelve-year-old brother, John, grabbed a falling fly brush and became "one of the most efficient fly fanners in the procession." They thought of their Uncle Wilson, who must have been in this battle, and went to look for him. They found out he'd been captured at Kennesaw Mountain, taken to Camp Chase Prison in Ohio as a prisoner of war and died there of smallpox.

The bullets fell thickly in the yard of the Atlanta Medical College, where Dr. Noel P.P. D'Alvigny was operating. His daughter Pauline was a lifelong friend of Sarah's mother. Pauline was assisting her father and narrowly escaped being hit several times.

That night they retreated to the rock-walled basement of Richard Peters's flour mill. They needed safety from the shelling, since there was no bombproof shelter at the Shearers' house. The more furious the firing, the bigger the crowd in the basement grew. "Like an electric storm going over," the shelling seldom lasted more than an hour at a time.

Sarah's mother thought they'd be safer at home, so they gathered up animals and possessions and started home. The cows broke loose when they heard the sound of pickets firing. One cow found its way home, the other to an acquaintance's house. Not long afterward, her mother bought butter from this man. It turned out to be butter from her own cow. The man was forced to give the cow back.

Her father worried about his family being in the "shell infested danger zone" and obtained a furlough to go home. The city was almost completely surrounded by Sherman's army, and it was dangerously hard for him to get to his family. He made it home and packed up his family to travel to Social Circle to stay with an old great-uncle. He left to go north to Virginia, and they left to go east to Social Circle. They had to ford the South River. Sarah commented she was the first to cross and get to her great-uncle's, but that people usually dress to go somewhere. She had to undress after she got there, out of her wet clothes.

Little did they know that Social Circle was in the direct path of Sherman's march. When the Federal army approached, Sarah's mother hid the boys under the flooring of the backroom. For some mysterious reason Great-Uncle Jack's property was not bothered, although they could see the men marching and the fires burning all around. She described the sound of fireworks as the "mighty army" looked for its supper.

Her aunt, Mrs. John Floyd Huff, took refuge with her mother and grandmother to Social Circle. Worried about the approaching Yankees, they put little ninety-nine-year-old Granny to bed on top of the family papers, letters and valuables. The soldiers were told that Granny was very ill, and if they bothered her at all, that would certainly kill her. Little Granny, still very spry, took offense, hopped out of bed and shouted, "Why Effie, what do you mean! I'm not sick and I'm going into the yard to see why the chickens are making such a fuss." The ruse was over; the house was ransacked until the soldiers discovered the bee gums. The bees swarmed and stung the soldiers so dreadfully that they made a quick exit and never came back.

These are some of the delightful memories of Sarah Huff, who is buried at Oakland Cemetery.

CHAPTER 7

The Jewish Section

They are not dead who live in the hearts of their loved ones.
—Inscription from the Cohen plot

INTRODUCTION

By the early 1800s half of America's Jewish population lived in the South. German-born Jewish families date back to 1847 in Marthasville. The Jacob Haas family was the first to arrive. With Henry Levi, Jacob opened up a dry goods store in Decatur. The family lived above the store. Their daughter Caroline was born on November 14, 1848, making her the first Atlanta baby, as Julia Withers was actually born in Marietta. A matter of semantics? Caroline later married another Jacob Haas. The father Jacob moved to Philadelphia and left his business to David Mayer, an early Atlanta pioneer.

By 1860, the German Jewish population in Atlanta reached fifty, and the community needed a burial place. In 1869, David Mayer bought fifteen plots at Oakland for the Hebrew Benevolent Congregation. Death and marriage call for a rabbi. Once a full-time rabbi moved to Atlanta, the congregation evolved into a full-fledged synagogue, which eventually became the temple.

After 1885, Atlanta's German Jews were joined by a wave of Jewish immigrants from Russia and Eastern Europe. They soon outnumbered the German Jews and formed their own strictly orthodox synagogue, Ahavath Achim. In order to procure money for their various projects, the Atlanta Ladies Memorial Association sold some of their extra plots to the temple, which in turn sold one quarter of the plots to the Ahavath Achim congregation. In Eastern European Jewish style, the graves were spaced close together, packing in as many occupants as they could with no walkways, in order to maximize the space. This section looks like a city of skyscrapers

Wide-angled view of the new Jewish section for Jews of Eastern European descent. They were buried in Eastern orthodox tradition. *Photo by Eric Gaare.*

and is the most easily identifiable section at Oakland. In contrast, the temple plots blend in. The more settled Jewish families from the pioneer days wanted to emulate their Christian neighbors and burial practices.

THE RICH BROTHERS

You always like to see nice people do well.

Morris Rich (Reich) was thirteen years old when he came to America from his native Kashau, Hungary. He came with his older brother William, penniless and almost illiterate. His first job was working as a clerk in a store in Cleveland, Ohio. Then he moved south to Chattanooga and later Albany to start his own business. He had to travel to his customers and longed for the day when they would travel to him.

He liked the South and was impressed by Atlanta. In postwar Atlanta, new buildings were going up everywhere. Atlanta's population jumped over 100 percent. It was a city on the way up, and his brother William was already there. Borrowing $500 from his older brother, Morris opened a retail store on Whitehall Street. It was 1867, and there were mud holes in front of the store. He covered them with loose boards and opened for business, first with brother Emanuel and later with brother Daniel. This was a family-oriented and family-run business from the start.

In the early days, when he was bidding for the farm trade, Morris allowed farmers to barter for their purchases with eggs, corn and other farm products. People would come from miles away. He radicalized the retail business by advertising one price for every customer, with the price based on the value of the product. Anyone not satisfied with the product could return it. These were innovative changes.

Early ads were startlingly precise: ladies' white cotton hose, ten cents; French kid gloves with one button, fifty cents; with two buttons, seventy-five cents. The prime seller at the store was the fifty-cent corset.

The first year's sales topped $5,000 and there were five employees. The business kept on growing. Morris installed the first plate-glass windows in an Atlanta store. Rich's became the first store to be departmentalized, which angered its customers at first. The old patrons had their favorite clerks and wanted to be waited on by them, regardless of what department the article came from.

By 1901, the store had twice been added on to, with one annex that was six stories high and housed an elevator. Rich's became an Atlanta institution. In the late 1920s–early 1930s, when Atlanta was rocked by the Depression, the Atlanta school system was bankrupt and couldn't pay its teachers. Walter Rich, Morris's nephew, suggested that the teachers be paid in scrip, then they could trade the scrip for money or products at Rich's, as the department store still had money. When the school system had money again, it could pay Rich's back. And it did—all $645,000. "We tell our employees we want them to do something for Atlanta," said cousin Dick Rich, and "we must practice what we preach." Rich's also paid policemen's salaries during that time.

While Morris was vacationing in Atlantic City in 1928, he died suddenly. He was eighty-one years old. The store was closed all day that Saturday to honor him, the founder of the oldest retail establishment in the Southeast. Rich's sales topped $647 million in 1985 with seventeen stores. Customer satisfaction, novel in 1867, was always the basic creed at Rich's Department Store.

The brothers are buried in the family plot in Oakland's Jewish section, with modest markers and a bench for visitors. You always like to see nice people do well.

Joseph Jacobs and the First Coca-Cola

The story of how Coca-Cola came to be starts with pharmacist John Pemberton (not buried at Oakland) of Columbus, Georgia, where he settled after the Civil War. His severe war wound led him to morphine addiction, a common problem among Civil War veterans. He studied medicine with Samuel Thompson, who was not a bloodletter, but rather an herbalist who made his own medicinal cures. Patented medicines from that time had dubious value. By today's standards, they would be called "snake oil," but experimenting with herbs and concoctions to help soothe various pains helped lead to the birth of the Coca-Cola formula.

In his laboratory in Columbus, Pemberton mixed and sold his medicines and cosmetic products. He began to work on a coca (a leaf that contains cocaine) and cola nut beverage mix that was intended to stop headaches, calm nerves and serve as a pain reliever for himself and other war vets. He moved to Atlanta, where he mixed the coca cola formula in a three-legged pot in his backyard. On May 8, 1886, he took a sample to Joseph Jacobs Pharmacy on Marietta and Peachtree Streets, in the heart of downtown Atlanta, to test the product. The urban myth goes that Jacobs's fountain man, Willis Venable, accidentally mixed it with carbonated water instead of ice water. They drank it and loved it and began to serve the five-cent drink at Joseph Jacobs's Pharmacy, along with root beer and ginger ale. Not only was it "Delicious and Refreshing," but Pemberton also pushed it as a cure for headaches, nerves, hangovers, queasy stomachs and morphine addiction (or at least a substitute for it). It's well known that Pemberton never reaped the great financial rewards from the Coca-Cola boon, dying nearly penniless.

Although the Coca-Cola fortune also eluded Joe Jacobs, he was far from penniless, operating over sixteen successful drugstores in Atlanta with links in every section of the city. Dr. Joseph Jacobs, twenty-eight years younger than Pemberton, lived in Athens, Georgia, before moving to Atlanta. When he was fifteen, he became an apprentice and lifelong admirer of Dr. Crawford Long, the discoverer of ether anesthesia. Dr. Long was not only Joseph Jacobs's mentor, but also his financial angel, assisting him with chemistry schooling at the University of Georgia and the Philadelphia College of Pharmacy.

Joe established a drug business in Athens, being one of the few licensed pharmacists in Georgia. He gathered his own herbs, like Queen's Delight or Prince Pine Roots, from neighboring fields to brew into tonics, stocking his drugstore cabinets with these and the standard medicines of the day. He moved to Atlanta, which had a population of fifty thousand in 1884, buying out Walter A. Taylor's business. It was at that Five Points drugstore that Coca-Cola history was made.

Jacobs was well known for making retail prices at his store lower than his competitors, advertising his store as the "Birthplace of Cut Prices." What others sold for $20, he advertised for $19.99. His ads were on the front page of the *Atlanta Journal* until newspaper policy changed to allow only news on the front page. He moved his ads to the middle, full-page ads too, the first ever in Atlanta.

He also wrote a biography of his mentor—Dr. Crawford Long—was an avid fan of the Scottish poet Robert Burns and organized the Burns Club in Atlanta. His collection of "Burnsiana" items was the finest in America. He was also well known for his Civil War collection. He once had a dinner party where literary giants James Whitcomb Riley, Joel Chandler Harris and Bill Arp all sat at the same table.

Jacobs died at the age of seventy and is buried in a mausoleum at Oakland.

Jacob Elsas and Cabbagetown

Jacob Elsas of Württemberg, Germany, arrived in America in the 1840s, penniless but not unskilled, coming from a family of weavers, dyers and dealers in cotton goods. He met someone onboard the boat to America who lent him one dollar so he could go to Cincinnati to find work with an uncle who had a business there. And so he did. After the Civil War, he moved South to Cartersville, Georgia, rented a log cabin and opened a store. Later he built a brick store across from the courthouse.

In 1869 his attention centered on Atlanta, where he started out as a rag dealer and junk trader. His full-page ad in the City Directory read:

Elsas and Brother
Paper Rag And Hide
the Highest Price in Cash Paid for Dried Fruit and
Old News and Book Paper, Loose Cotton, Fur skins, Beeswax,
Tallow, Ginseng, Feathers, Scrap Iron, Old Metal, etc.

With capital from his uncle, Elsas went from retail into manufacturing, first as Elsas, May and Co.; then as the Southern Bag Factory; then with a charter from the state to start a spinning mill, the Fulton Cotton Spinning Company. The first year the company made 1,000 spindles a day, which increased to 100,000 at the height of the mill's production years. As the Fulton Bag and

The mausoleum of Joe Jacobs, owner of the pharmacy where the first Coca-Cola was served. *Photo by Eric Gaare.*

Cotton Mills, the company made bags for agricultural products. The mills became one of the largest textile manufacturing companies in the world.

But Jacob Elsas himself is perhaps best known for his philanthropic contributions to Atlanta, especially in the developing of Georgia Tech, Grady Hospital and the Hebrew Orphans Home. When Elsas appropriated $65,000 for the creation of an Atlanta School of Technology, someone asked, "What's a School of Technology?" Elsas answered, "We are selling our old raw materials at $5 a ton to states that have trained engineers who fabricate it and sell it back to us for $75 to $100 a ton. I have to send my son to Massachusetts Institute of Technology to learn to do this." That was one thing a school of technology in Atlanta could provide.

In 1925, when Elsas was eighty-two years old, he became concerned about the need for a pay ward at the new Grady Hospital. Grady already served the poor of the city, but what about the "people of small means who are independent in mind and would not accept charity?" When an unexpected illness occurred, they would be facing heavy financial burdens from hospital costs. A pay ward would set hospital costs at affordable prices for working-class families.

Known as the humanitarian with the big heart, Jacob Elsas died in 1932 at the age of ninety. He was buried in the Elsas mausoleum on a hill, close to the Memorial Drive wall in the newer Jewish section of Oakland. There's a back window in the mausoleum, as legend goes, so that Jacob can look out and oversee the operations at the mill. Although the mill hasn't operated since the 1970s, he can see how the building has been renovated into upscale lofts that house area artists, musicians and businessmen. He would also take pride in the fact that his mill building was placed on the National Register of Historic Places in 1976.

Cabbagetown

Cabbagetown was built as a mill town for the Fulton Bag and Cotton Mills, situated on the other side of the fence from Oakland's Potter's Field. When the mills began operating in 1881, the workforce, consisting mostly of poor whites from the north Georgia mountains, needed a place to live.

Jacob Elsas built a small community of one- and two-story shotgun houses, a style of house popular in the South from 1880 to 1930. Typically wooden framed and simple in design, they consist of three to four rooms, with a modest front porch. The name derived from the fact that when the rooms were lined up just so, you could fire a gun straight through the front door and out the rear without hitting anything.

At its height, the mills had a workforce of almost three thousand. A strike in 1915 failed to unionize them. They called their community Cabbagetown, and it was a tightly knit, semi-isolated, homogeneous community of people whose lives centered on the mills. When the mills closed in 1977, the neighborhood went into a steep decline. In the late 1990s it was revitalized, rebuilt and restructured into lofts and restaurants. The neighborhood now sponsors two annual festivals: the annual Cabbagetown reunion, known as "the Vegetable," is held in the summertime, and the "Chomp and Stomp" takes place in November.

As to the name Cabbagetown—where did it come from? There are at least three varying explanations or legends that explain the name. One story says that the mountain folks who worked at the mills, being of mainly Scots-Irish descent, grew cabbages in their front yards. The smell of cooking cabbage is quite distinctive, and the name might have been used derisively by bordering neighbors. Another story says that a train carrying a load of cabbages derailed near the village and the poor millworkers poured forth to gather the cabbages and used them in every meal. Another legend says a Model T was making a sharp turn through the narrow streets of Cabbagetown, flipped over and spilled its cargo of cabbages into the street.

Mockingbird sitting on top of the marker for Potter's Field. The Old Fulton Bag and Cotton Mill and Cabbagetown can be seen in the background. *Photo by Eric Gaare.*

Someone yelled, "Cabbages, free cabbages," and the rush to get to the vegetables ensued. As payment for the free cabbages, the Model T was rolled back onto its tires and took off.

All in all, the smell of cooking cabbage is highly recognizable. It can stay on the stove cooking all day, as long as the water doesn't boil out, making the cabbage softer and softer and sending out that distinct odor.

LUCILLE SELIG FRANK AND THE LEO FRANK MURDER TRIAL

"The Frank saga has not lost its power to haunt," said Steve Olney in his 2003 book about the 1913 trial of Leo Frank, who was convicted of strangling thirteen-year-old Mary Phagan of Marietta at the Pencil Factory, where she was an employee and he was co-owner and manager. He was a New York Jew. She was a beautiful, innocent young girl from a "cracker" family.

On the afternoon of April 26, 1913, Mary went to the factory on her way to the Confederate Memorial Day Parade to pick up her paycheck.

She was never seen alive again. A night watchman discovered her body in the factory basement early the next morning. She had been beaten, assaulted and strangled. Leo Frank became the primary suspect. The other suspect was a black janitor who had also been present in the building the day of the murder. The ensuing trial became a nationally publicized, highly sensationalized one that brought out the worst in those involved, and in some cases the best. Anti-Semitism and the Ku Klux Klan reared their ugly heads. Everyone had an opinion about this case. Most thought Leo Frank was guilty. It was a dark time for the state's judicial system. The defense of Leo Frank was labeled the most ill-conducted defense in the history of Georgia jurisdiction. The trial gained notoriety because the words of a black man were used to convict a white man.

It was so big a story that I've placed it in three sections of this book. This section features the story of the trial and the story of Lucille Selig Frank, Leo's wife. In the "Women at Oakland" section, you'll read the story of Sarah Grant Slaton, the wife of the governor of Georgia, John Slaton, who had Leo Frank's sentence commuted from death to life. In the "Famous, Infamous or Should-be Famous" section, you'll read about Governor John Marshall Slaton's part in the case. All three are buried at Oakland.

Leo Frank was found guilty of the murder of Mary Phagan and sentenced to death. In 1915, Georgia Governor John Marshall Slaton used his gubernatorial power to stay the death sentence and commute it to life. His decision created an angry outburst not heard of before in the state, angering twenty-six Marietta men, many of whom were in prominent positions, who stormed the Milledgeville Prison Farm (where Frank was recovering from an almost fatal knife wound to the throat, courtesy of another prisoner). The mob kidnapped Frank, cut the prison telephone lines and drove 175 miles to Frey's Gin in Marietta, where they lynched him from an oak tree and in clear view of the Phagan home. His last words were, "I think more of my wife and mother than I do of my own life." He asked that his wedding ring be given to his wife, Lucille.

Lucille Selig Frank, Atlanta born and bred, the daughter of Emil and Josephine Selig of the Selig Chemical Company/National Linen Company, wed Leo Frank on November 30, 1910. Three years later, she sat close behind her husband during the twenty-nine-day trial for his life. She was unwavering in her belief in her husband's innocence and integrity, saying to the press, "He ever has been just the plain, more or less studious and serious minded Leo, gentle and thoughtful, sincere and true." After his conviction, she fought for the next two years to save him from execution, writing letters to friends and people in prominent places, like Governor Slaton, and issuing pleas in newspapers throughout the country to help her husband. One appeared in the Green Bay, Wisconsin *Gazette*: "I beg the American people to save my husband's life because he is innocent. Mrs. Leo M. Frank."

She signed her letters to Frank while he was in prison with "Lots of love and kisses my sweetheart, goodnight and may God bless you. Lovingly, your own Honey." When he was stabbed in prison and almost bled to death, she was there to nurse him and bring him freshly cooked meals. Leo wrote to a friend, "It was indeed providential that my dear wife was here when I was so grievously hurt. She has been a pillar of strength to me. She spends 8–10 hours daily with me." But she was in Atlanta and he in Milledgeville on the night of August 17, 1915, when he was abducted and lynched.

In her only public statement about the lynching, Lucille stated to a reporter for the *Augusta Chronicle* on October 1, 1915,

> *I am a Georgia girl, born and reared in this state, and educated in her schools. I am a Jewess; some will throw that in my face, I know, but I have no apologies to make for my religion. I am also a Georgian, and American, and I do not apologize for that either…I only pray that those who destroyed Leo's life will realize the truth before they meet their God—they perhaps are not entirely to blame, fed as they were on lies unspeakable, their passion aroused by designing persons. Some of them, I am sure, did not realize the horror of their act. But those who inspired these men to this unlawful act, what of them? Will not their consciences make for them a hell on Earth, and will not their associates, in their hearts, despise them?*

Lucille would speak no more of the trial. She was only twenty-seven, embittered, somewhat reclusive. In 1916, she went to Tennessee, where a brother-in-law offered her a job in a women's clothing shop. In the 1920s she returned to Atlanta, where she worked at the glove counter at J.P. Allen's Clothing Store, managed by a brother-in-law. She never remarried and always signed her name "Mrs. Leo Frank." Although she functioned outwardly, those close to her believed she never stopped mourning for her husband, who was buried far away from Atlanta, in Mount Carmel Cemetery, Queens, New York. Dr. James Kauffman, an internist who treated her, said, "She somatized her complaints. She had chest pains, headaches. When I think of her, I think of depression. Leo might have been killed, but she served a life sentence."

She died in 1957 of heart disease, forty-two years after Leo's murder. She was cremated. She wanted her ashes scattered in a public park in Atlanta, but a statute prevented her relatives from granting her wish. Her ashes remained in a cardboard box at Patterson's Funeral Home for several years. It was a time of strong anti-Semitism in Atlanta, climaxed by the

Lucille Selig Frank's small angel denotes the only marker for her grave, which was secretly dug between her parents, Josephine and Emil Selig. *Photo by Robert Gaare.*

bombing at the Jewish Temple in 1958. Fearing more repercussions, the family knew they were asking for trouble if they placed her remains in a publicly marked grave. Her ashes rode in her nephew Allan Marcus's car trunk for six months before he and his brother went to Oakland at dawn. Using garden tools, they dug a hole for Lucille's ashes between the graves of her parents in the Jewish section and buried her remains there. No marker was ever placed, but if you find the site in the new Jewish section, you'll see that someone has placed a small angel statue where her ashes lie between her parents' markers.

CHAPTER 8

The Oakland Women

*I have returned 51 times since my first visit to Oakland. I have not yet seen
everything…The stone angels warm my heart…I am mystified that the sound of an
acorn falling will lead my eyes to a marker I have never noticed before, and the words
will say something that I need to hear.*
—Rosalind Hillhouse, Oakland tour guide

SARAH FRANCES GRANT JACKSON SLATON

It was November 19, 1891, and Sarah Frances Grant married Thomas
Cobb Jackson at St. Philips Cathedral in Atlanta. It was the most
impressive and notable wedding ceremony Atlanta had ever witnessed: the
merger of two prominent Atlanta families. The bride's jewelry alone was
enough to make one gawk: an exquisite pin encrusted with diamonds, the
center a priceless pearl and two emeralds on either side; pear-shaped pearls
for a pendant (gift of the groom); earrings made of large diamond solitaires
(gift of the groom's parents); the necklace a chain of many diamonds, each
a matchless stone (gift of her grandmother).

These two young people had been well known in social circles. Sarah
was the only daughter of Colonel W.D. Grant, was a descendant of the
Grants, Reeds and Cobbs and was called "a flower of the Old South as
well as of the new—one of the most attractive and loveable women who
has ever graced Atlanta society." The groom, Tom Jackson, had the blood
of the Jacksons, Davenports and Cobbs in his veins. This brilliant young
man already had "everything in the way of wealth and position, personally
a charmingly attractive man, his friends worth having, his admirers many."
The newlyweds were off to a honeymoon in New York, followed by a tour
of Europe.

The dream became a nightmare fifteen months later when Thomas
Cobb Jackson, while in a hack parked in front of his father's house, put a

The Grant mausoleum that contains the remains of Governor John Marshall Slaton and his wife, Sarah Frances Grant Slaton. Bell Tower Ridge. *Photo by Robert Gaare.*

bullet to his head and died instantly. His name had been linked with Lewis Redwine and the Gate City Bank foreclosure. But posthumously, he was never found guilty of any crime. He was buried in the family cemetery in Athens, Georgia, leaving his young widow in shock.

A few years later, Sallie Fannie (her nicknames) Grant Jackson was introduced to John "Jack" Slaton, her brother's college roommate, at a dance at the Opera House. They wrote many love notes and were married at her parents' home on Peachtree Street on July 12, 1898.

Sarah always came down to eat breakfast with her husband, just as she had growing up with her father, Colonel William D. Grant. That's the way she started her days, at any hour that suited either one of them. If she failed to have breakfast with her father or husband, days might have passed with their busy schedules preventing them from seeing each other. Her father was one of the most scholarly men of his day and the wealthiest, and they loved to talk about books, literature and articles in the paper.

In 1912, Sarah became Georgia's first lady as the wife of Governor John Marshall Slaton, and her days were filled with many civic duties. Then came the Leo Frank trial and Frank's conviction. Governor Slaton was asked to review the case. It was a time of serious soul-searching for him. Sarah anxiously awaited his decision. He reportedly said, "I fear I'll make a widow of you the second time" (referring to the untimely death of her first husband and his probable one if he commuted Frank's death sentence). Governor Slaton decided to commute the sentence to life imprisonment. She kissed him and said, "I would rather be the widow of a brave and honorable man than the wife of a coward." He later credited her with giving him the strength to follow his conscience.

Sarah died in 1945, ten years prior to her husband—she was not a twice-widowed woman after all. She was much loved and respected, known throughout the state for her charm, character and good deeds. She rests with her second husband in the Grant mausoleum at Oakland.

SARAH KUGLER DYE AND JOHN MORGAN DYE

In July of 1864, Atlanta was bombarded with shells from the Confederate and Union armies. It was the middle of the Atlanta campaign, and both sides were fighting for possession of the Gate City of the South. The campaign would continue for another month before General John Bell Hood and the Rebel forces pulled out and General William T. Sherman and the Union forces pulled in.

Sarah Dye was alone with four children in their home on the corner of Baker and Ivy Streets. It was built by her husband Thomas, said to be the best carpenter and framer in Atlanta. Now Thomas was off to war, even though he was reluctant to do so. Sarah and the children dug a bombproof shelter in the side of the hill of the backyard and settled in, hoping to survive the daily shelling. Her nearly two-year-old son John Morgan (named for the Confederate raider from Kentucky) took sick around the time of the Battle of Atlanta, July 20, 1864. She carried Johnny off to get help for him, leaving the four-year-old Joseph Edward and the nine-year-old James Buchannon in the care of twelve-year-old Maranda.

Sarah came upon a Union doctor who gave her some medicine for the sick child. She asked how she should measure out the medicine when it was so dark in their dugout. He taught her the trick of pouring the medicine into a spoon, placing her finger in the spoon and when the liquid reached a certain place on her finger, she'd know it was the right amount. Right amount or not, John died and Sarah needed to bury him. She had already lost two children before the war, who were buried in the family plot at Oakland. She did what she had to do: she found a box to place John in and carried him off to Oakland Cemetery.

While on her way, she encountered an unidentified black man pulling a dray. He asked where she was going. She replied and he answered, "Lady you got no business being alone to bury a child and being by yourself on the streets." So he helped her, taking them all to Oakland, helping her dig the grave and bury the boy. As he was traveling in the opposite direction, he could not take her back home. Spent and weary, Sarah fell asleep on her small child's grave. When she awoke, she started back for home, trying to avoid the "red fireballs," relying on the strength a woman can muster for the sake of her family.

According to the "Southern Claims Papers," issued after the war to help reimburse Southerners for their wartime losses, Sarah was a Union woman and against the war from start to finish. She had made it public that she thought the war would "bring no good." She was labeled a Union sympathizer, even though her husband served in the Confederate army. (Apparently he was conscripted, forced to join and often went AWOL.) When General Sherman gave the orders that Atlanta was to be evacuated, Sarah had three choices: stay and find work, go South or sign the oath of allegiance and go North. Those who signed the oath would receive food and assistance from the Union. She went North, at least to Cincinnati, and then to Alabama where she had relatives. Finally she returned to Atlanta the summer after the war's end.

When she returned home, she found the house destroyed, along with the outer buildings. There was only an empty lot and part of a fence post. Her

John Morgan Dye's grave. He was the two-year-old son of Sarah Dye, who buried her son during the Battle of Atlanta. Original six acres. *Photo by Eric Gaare.*

husband Thomas came home after the war and built a new house. They eventually sold this one and moved to another house on Marietta Street. Sarah had three more children after the war. She died in 1888 of cancer, and Thomas died in 1890 from a fall off a ladder.

The Dye lot at Oakland is a fourteen-grave lot, full of family members and one outsider. You'll find Sarah's marker (still legible); John Morgan's marker; that of a son Mintory, who died at the age of three in 1855; Ella and George Toney (daughter and son-in-law); Connie C. Floyd (Ella's daughter); and Lula B. Holmes (not a family member). There is no stone to mark Thomas's grave, or the son Joseph Edward or two daughters born after the war. Daughter Maranda Dye Hill is also buried in the plot. She was supposedly the beauty of the family and died during childbirth in 1877. The last son, James, is buried with his family in Texas. There's also said to be an infant daughter, Loueza, born in 1849, who's reportedly buried under the steps. Great-granddaughter Patricia Scheff said she remembers her grandmother Ella Toney telling her to avoid that first step when visiting the gravesite, as a family member was buried there. The last occupant, Lula B. Holmes, was a widow and friend of Margaret and George Toney, parents of Pat Scheff. Lula had no plot of her own, and they offered her the last spot in the Dye lot at Oakland.

This story is one of the most powerfully poignant stories told at Oakland and is a favorite stop on the Oakland tour. Many thanks to Patricia Scheff for sharing the details and stories she heard from her grandmother, Ella Dye Toney, whose mother was the unforgettable Sarah Dye.

CARRIE STEELE LOGAN

The mother of orphans, she hath done what she could.

Born into slavery and orphaned as a child, native Georgian Carrie Steele managed to learn how to read and write, which were uncommon skills for a slave to have. After being freed, she worked as a matron at the Atlanta Union Railroad Depot. Every day she viewed hungry, half-clad, ignorant black children who lived on the streets, the aftereffects of the Civil War. She took pity on them.

During the day she found an old boxcar where they could take shelter and play safely. At night she brought them to her modest two-bedroom cottage on Wheat Street. But the number of orphaned children she took in continued to grow and grow, while her house did not. She wrote the story of her life and sold her autobiography to help her with the big project she

Carrie Steele Logan's grave. She was the mother of Atlanta's African American orphans. Her husband Josehia's grave is the smaller one. African American grounds. *Photo by Robert Gaare.*

had in mind. No known copy of this book is still extant. After receiving a charter from the city council in 1888 for the Carrie Steele Orphans' Home, she went about soliciting more funds for land and a building, selling her own home in the process to add to the funds. With $5,000 and four acres of land, she was able to erect a three-story brick orphanage, dedicated in 1892, the oldest black orphanage in the city of Atlanta.

She married, at the age of sixty, Josehia Logan, a fine Christian gentleman and a minister from New York, and the two of them became parents to fifty orphaned black children. No longer uncouth and ignorant, the children were trained for the service industry and educated at the orphanage. Each day started off in prayer, to help place necessary "stepping stones for the betterment of the race." The older girls were taught domestic and "fancy" work. The boys were taught farm work. They all learned to read and recite Bible verses. Carrie's intent was not just to give the children food and shelter, but also to keep them from a life of crime and the Georgia chain gang, and to prepare them for lives as contributing adults.

Resigning her depot job, Carrie gave herself fully to the orphanage, which she called "the greatest joy of my life." She died in 1900, her husband carrying on her work until his death. The orphanage, still in existence, is called the Carrie Steele-Pitts Home, Pitts after the name of the second director, Clara Maxwell Pitts, who served for forty years. Now in its third location on Fairburn Road and under the direction of Olivette Anderson, the fourth director, the home serves around one hundred at-risk, abandoned, neglected or orphaned black children. Under the wings of the United Way, the home has a new addition, the Allison Life Learning Center, complete with indoor pool, gym, chapel, classrooms and a computer lab.

Carrie Steele Logan received a 1998 award as a Georgia Woman of Achievement. She hath done what she could.

GUSSIE HILL THOMPSON

Once thought of as the most beautiful woman in Atlanta, Gussie Hill Thompson died of consumption in 1878. The *Daily Constitution* described her death thusly: "On the above evening she slept easily and pleasantly until an early hour next morning when she awoke with a choking sensation, after which she passed away from life calmly and peaceably." She was at the house of Georgia Governor Alfred H. Colquitt, who was a distant relative. Described as the devoted wife of Joseph Thompson Jr. of the firm of Cox, Hill, and Thompson, Gussie was the daughter-in-law of colorful, loud-talking Atlanta pioneer and hotel- and saloonkeeper Dr. Joseph Thompson.

As Gussie had been afflicted with consumption for some time, her death was expected. She was only thirty-four. She had been sent to various medicinal spas for recreation and medical treatments, but to no avail. Her funeral cortege arrived at Wesley Chapel on March 20, 1878, to find it full, with fifty former slaves and current house servants of the family, the joint choir of the church and Gussie's own Beethoven Society Chorale, plus many church members. Governor Colquitt himself delivered the eulogy, described as one of the finest and most beautiful eulogies ever given. There wasn't a dry eye in the house.

As the procession left the church and moved down the streets toward Oakland Cemetery, the new bell of the Tallulah Fire Engine Company tolled in her honor. The bell had been named for her after she received the second highest number of votes among the ladies at the Ladies Fair of 1867. The fair was a fundraiser for Fire Company #1, which needed a new steam pumping engine and a fire alarm bell. The ladies of the town came to the rescue, raising the much-needed $999.35. A gallant gentleman came through with the extra $0.65 to round out the proceeds. A candy bell was hung as a centerpiece around the ballot boxes where the money and

The grave of sleeping beauty Gussie Hill Thompson, one of the most beautiful crypts at Oakland. Bell Tower Ridge. *Photo by Robert Gaare.*

the votes were collected. The young lady with the highest number of votes, Miss Emma Latimer, won the honor of having the new steamer named after her. She declined, saying a steam engine needed a stronger name, and recommended Castalia, a fabled land in classical literature where no one ever grows old. Miss Augusta Hill received the second highest number of votes and the honor of having the bell named after her.

The bell arrived, weighing in at one ton, on August 1, 1867. The *Daily Intelligencer*'s article about the event was titled "Distinguished Arrival." The inscription on the bell read:

Dedicated to the Public Service
in honor of
Miss Augusta Hill
July, 1867

Alas, Gussie was not in town on August 8 at the dedication ceremony and could not ring the bell for the first time. After that day it rang out every time there was a fire, indicating the approximate location of the fire by the number of rings, coordinating with the number of the ward. It also rang out when Benjamin Harvey Hill died in 1882; when Alexander Stephens died in 1883; and of course when its beautiful namesake, Augusta Hill Thompson, died in 1878.

Her aboveground stone crypt stands alone at Oakland between the Herndon/Hill mausoleum and the Kiser mausoleum. It reminds me of Sleeping Beauty's crypt, and is carved with stone roses and vines. Her beauty now sleeps through the ages.

MARY GLOVER THURMAN: THE ANGEL OF ATLANTA

Dr. Fendall D. Thurman brought his Virginia belle bride to Atlanta, Georgia. It was 1855 and they were a pioneer family. Dr. Thurman saw the potential in this quiet little village, set up his dental practice and developed a reputation as one of the best dentists in the South, and also the wealthiest.

They had a beautiful home on West Peachtree Street, where they both were avid gardeners. In his retirement, the "eccentric" doctor and his wife kept a greenhouse where they grew some of the most beautiful flowers in the city.

After Dr. Thurman died in 1896, Mary lived alone with her maid and twenty-five-year companion, Katie, whom she had raised as if her own. Her only child, Wiley Dickerson Thurman, died in 1865 at the age of five. She refused to sell her grand home, deriving pleasure from the thousands of flowers in her garden. Her jonquils and hyacinths were said to be particularly fine. She loved to pick flowers and give them to neighbors or sick friends and strangers, to brighten their rooms. She was dubbed the Angel of Atlanta for spreading flowery cheer to Atlanta's hospitals.

She died a wealthy woman at the age of eighty-seven, outliving her husband for twenty years. Now she resides at Oakland under one of the most beautiful memorial statues to adorn any grave there. It is one of the most photographed too. Carved in relief, an angel sits with outspread wings and arms on a bench of carved flowers and vines. The design is said to be a copy of a Chester French work. Visitors to Oakland often ask to see *The Copy*. They are referring to this statue.

After her death, Mary's beautiful home was razed to build the Biltmore Hotel. Many of the Thurmans' fine trees were left standing. A beautiful outdoor terrace and rear gardens serve as reminders of her love of flowers and her generosity in sharing them.

"The Angel of Atlanta," Mary Glover Thurman, said to be a copy of a Daniel Chester French relief sculpture of the Kinsley Monument in Woodlawn Cemetery, New York. Bell Tower Ridge. *Photo by Eric Gaare.*

NIOBE

Niobe is one of the most tragic tales told in Greek mythology. She is the stock figure of a mother in mourning. She was the mortal wife of Amphion, king of Thebes, and the mother of fourteen children called the Niobids, seven sons and seven daughters. At the annual celebration in honor of the Greek goddess Leto, wife of Zeus and mother of twins Apollo and Artemis, Niobe bragged that she had much to be proud of. Her children were her pride and joy. She proclaimed the festival to be mere folly, as Leto had only two children and she had fourteen. Why should Leto be worshipped when she had seven times as many offspring? Leto was indignant at Niobe's hubris, her arrogance and excessive pride in claiming she, a mortal, was greater than a goddess. In Olympus, no arrogant claim by a mortal went unnoticed. Leto sent her two children to punish foolish Niobe. Apollo killed the seven sons with poisoned arrows and Artemis killed the seven daughters. Niobe was left with no children to brag of. Niobe cradled the last daughter and began to weep.

Some versions of the story say she wept herself to death. Others say she fled to Mount Sipylus and turned to stone as she wept. At Mount Sipylus

Niobe from Greek mythology was the stock figure for a mother in eternal mourning. She weeps at the Gray lot at Oakland. Bell Tower Ridge. *Photo by Robert Gaare.*

today, there is a rock carving of a female face that the locals say is Niobe. The stone appears to weep tears in the summer. Whatever story you believe, Niobe remains the symbol of eternal mourning as she weeps a never-ending flow of tears.

Her statue adorns the Gray plot and mourns over the deaths of James Richard Gray and Mary Inman Gray, who sat at the helm of the Gray dynasty of the *Atlanta Journal* from 1900 to 1939.

JULIA COLLIER HARRIS: NEWSPAPERWOMAN

In an age and section of the country where middle-class women were relegated to a largely domestic role, she demonstrated that a woman could have brains and use them, could carve out a career for herself outside the home, and could take a stand and fight for causes she believed in.
—Dictionary of Georgia Biography

She was a Collier and a Rawson, and in marriage a Harris—strong and prominent Atlanta pioneer lines merged in her veins. And she was a brilliant, risk taking newspaperwoman in her own right.

The Oakland Women

Tragedy struck her life many times. Her mother, Susie Julia Eliza Rawson, died shortly before Julia's 1897 marriage to Julian LaRose Chandler Harris, son of the well-known Joel Chandler Harris, of *Uncle Remus* fame. Her own father died tragically from an accidental gunshot wound in 1900. Her six younger siblings, ranging in age from seven to twenty-two, were left in her care after her father's death. In 1903–04, her own two children died within nine months of each other, four-year-old Charles and three-year-old Pierre.

But her marriage to Julian endured for sixty-five years. The two of them created a dynamic journalist force that rocked racially prejudiced Georgia in the 1920s and culminated in a Pulitzer Prize for both of them in 1926. Their dual journalistic careers led them to Paris, where Julia was one of two female journalists who witnessed the signing of the Treaty of Versailles. She translated a book of Rumanian folktales and penned the first biography of her famous father-in-law, Joel Chandler Harris. Her son Charles had the red hair, bright blue eyes and gentle mischievousness of his grandfather.

But it was when Julia and Julian bought the controlling shares of the Columbus, Georgia *Enquirer-Sun* that they rose to national prominence. Quietly, the two went to work on this small-town paper of seven thousand subscribers. She reviewed books and wrote feature and news articles, and he ruled over the editorial page. Out of those pages came comments and opinions that rocked sleepy Columbus, Georgia, and echoed throughout the South. The Harrises wrote:

> *The whole KuKuxKlan Kamelia Komedy is so foolish that one no longer wishes to protest against it because it is anti-Negro, anti-Jew, anti-Catholic, but rather it makes the people of all the South appear idiotic when they continue to accept seriously Klon-vocations and Klon-cilliums, and tolerate the fantastic ravings of men who are fattening on the money of deluded simpletons.*

Then they took on the racial prejudice in the South:

> *Mule Hicks, an ignorant 17 year old Negro, stole a mule worth less than $100. After serving 12 years of his 20 year sentence, he was still in the chain gang, and as a result of his treatment, attempted to escape. He was convicted of murder and sentenced to hang, although not a witness saw the killing. Mule Hicks is a negro. Compare him to this forger and thief who stole $140,000 of state money and was pardoned after serving four years of a five year term. He was white.*

The Rawson mausoleum that contains the remains of Julian LaRose Harris, his wife Julia Collier Harris and their two infant sons. Julia's mother was a Rawson. *Photo by Robert Gaare.*

Then they took on the Scopes monkey trial and the teaching of evolution by a Tennessee schoolteacher. The Columbus paper lost subscribers and went bankrupt. But the Harrises received the 1926 Pulitzer Prize for journalism for "disinterested and meritorious public service rendered in its brave and energetic fight." They were cited for contributing to the end of the convict lease system in Georgia and a call to stop the lynching violence of the Ku Klux Klan.

Blacks throughout the nation applauded the award, calling Julian (and Julia) Harris "the most righteous editor of the South in attacking evil racial and intellectual bigotry." And all this for the son of Joel Chandler Harris, whom many blacks thought wrote stories that mocked the black dialect and stole their folklore and heritage. (This opinion is not so loudly voiced today, with Harris given credit for saving and restoring these priceless tales.)

Julia retired in 1938 from newspaper writing and continued to serve as a mentor for young, up-and-coming writers. Her great-niece Penny Hart of Atlanta remembers her great-aunt from her own childhood. She especially remembers the round table in the hall that was full of little treasures that represented the characters from the Uncle Remus tales and were sent by fans all over the world. Penny described her great-aunt as a highly intellectual, serious-minded woman, "as strong as battery acid. No smelling salt lady," who was always one to encourage the talents of a gifted child, having lost her own children so young in life.

Julia might have pooh-poohed her own many accomplishments. At one time she most valued a prize she had received at the age of twelve for sewing her own tucked and ruffled pantalettes. However, we recognize her as a 1998 Georgia Woman of Achievement.

She and Julian are buried in the Rawson mausoleum at Oakland.

CHAPTER 9

Owners and Pets

*While you are so sweetly sleeping, free from life's sorrow and care, we wander around
oft times weeping, for we miss you everywhere.*
—Oakland inscription

MOLLY WEIMER AND TWEET

Molly (Frederica) Weimer and her pet mockingbird, Tweet, are the first
known owner/pet burials at Oakland. Tweet died in 1874 and Molly
in 1899 at the age of seventy-four.

When Tweet died, Molly requested a carved mockingbird for the pet's
headstone. The stonecutter couldn't use such a small stone or cut such a
small figure, having neither the tools nor the skill to do it, so he made a
lamb, a stock figure often used for infant markers. Thus a small lamb rests
on the grave of Tweet, Frederica Weimer's mockingbird, in an easy-to-
overlook corner site close to the bell tower.

Tweet is a very popular stop on Oakland's tours. Bev Center, known
Atlanta storyteller and Oakland lover, tells this true story of what happened
when she stopped by Tweet's gravesite to share his story with visitors: "As
I stood beside their graves telling a story of Mrs. Molly Weimer and her
beloved mockingbird, Tweet, we heard a fluttering of wings. Over our
heads flew a mockingbird who then perched on a branch of a little tree near
the graves." No doubt this local mockingbird didn't want to miss out on the
telling of his favorite Oakland story.

HERMAN BENJAMIN AND JIP

For fourteen years, Herman Benjamin and his dog Jip, a rat terrier that
could pass for a lap dog, were inseparable. When Herman went to his

Tweet the mockingbird and the lamb
that sits atop his grave, close to that of
his owner, Frederica Weimer. Knit Mill
section. *Photo by Robert Gaare.*

downtown drugstore, Benjamin and Cronheim's, Jip went with him. When
Herman traveled by train to Ocala, Florida, to visit relatives, Jip went with
him, traveling in a special pet carrier Herman handmade out of an old
suitcase with ventilation holes cut in. Herman always said he'd just as soon
put himself in the baggage car as have Jip separated from him. He lavished
attention on his dog as if he were his own son.

Herman Benjamin was born in Hiere Swerda, Prussia, on August 1,
1863, the youngest of eight children. His parents, fearing rising prejudice
against Jews by the government and military conscription, packed up their
children and sent them off to America to live a better life. Herman became a
druggist and, after moving to Atlanta, worked for Joseph Jacobs's Pharmacy
in 1885 and 1886. He was no doubt working there when the first Coca-Cola
drink was served up by Willis E. Venable at the soda fountain in May of
1886. In 1887, Herman started his own drugstore and later married Ruby
Steinheimer. They had one child, a daughter, in 1906, who according to her
marker at Oakland lived only a few days. And then Jip came into Herman's
life in 1917. The very intelligent Jip was Herman's beloved companion and
friend for the next fourteen years.

Jip died two and a half years before Herman died, in the winter of 1931.
Herman's death notice in the *Atlanta Journal* on August 24, 1933, proclaims
that Herman had Jip embalmed after his death and put in a special casket
of copper. Jip's remains were to be left at the mortuary until his master's

death, as Herman wanted to be buried with and beside Jip. On August 22, 1933, while standing in front of his drugstore, Herman suffered a fatal heart attack. He was seventy years old. The *Journal* article goes on to say the two caskets were interred side by side. Jip's dates were listed as February 20, 1917, to February 7, 1931. Herman's were listed as August 1, 1863, to August 22, 1933. Herman wrote an inscription for Jip on his casket that read, "Jip–my companion, friend. True, unfalteringly loyal, pathetically, lovingly. I will continue to show the sincerity of my love and care for you, even in death till my end, and then ever after too, sharing with you the eternal sleep beneath the same sod."

Family members tell a different story. According to Susan B. (Benjamin) Deaver, daughter of Julien Benjamin, who was a grand-nephew of Herman Benjamin, Jip and Herman are buried in the same casket. Susan's a well-known Atlanta storyteller, historical researcher and archivist who keeps detailed and well-documented family records. She grew up hearing that Jip had been "stuffed," and in an interview with her father before his death, heard the following about Herman and Jip.

Being the youngest of that line of Benjamins, Herman had outlived his siblings. Thus, the burial duty fell to the next generation. Herman's nephew Julien Benjamin Sr. (Susan's grandfather) along with Morris Moss, his brother-in-law, went to the mortuary to make the funeral arrangements for Herman and Jip. Julien knew of his uncle's wish to be buried with Jip. The funeral home mortician informed him that it was against the law to bury an animal in a human's casket, "but, I tell you, I've got some business to do in the front office, and here is your uncle's coffin and here is the little dog's remains that I've been storing for him. I'll be gone about ten minutes." As soon as he left, Julien and Morris took the hint and placed Jip in the coffin with Uncle Herman. Julien proudly reported that "somehow I think Uncle Herman knows and feels comforted." He had fulfilled the family promise to his uncle.

At Oakland, in the Benjamin plot, there is no marker for Jip or mention of him. Of Herman's immediate family, there's only the small headstone for the infant daughter (unnamed) and the marker for Herman on the Benjamin plot. Family historian Susan B. Deaver, however, knows the real story.

REID AMOS BENSON AND ADONIS'S JODIE

R.B. Coulter met Reid when he was a freshman at Georgia Tech, Reid being his Sunday school teacher at First Baptist Church and a fine and popular teacher at that, always allowing everyone a chance to speak his mind. After R.B. graduated, the Sunday school class members stayed in touch. When R.B. returned to Atlanta in 1981, Reid had already had his dog, Jodie, for a couple of years. She was a dog with papers, a registered miniature schnauzer, well behaved and well trained by her master. But she was a one-man dog.

The two were a daily fixture in the Ansley Mall area during their early morning and evening walks. Reid was a history buff and one of the few people known to have read Franklin Garrett's massive *Environs of Atlanta* volumes from cover to cover. He became involved with Oakland, volunteering as a tour guide and serving on the board. Jodie would often accompany him on the tours. One morning she was ill when Reid awoke, and she died en route to the veterinarian. She was cremated and put in a biodegradable urn.

Reid secured a plot at Oakland for himself and asked the sexton if they could bury Jodie's urn at the foot of his plot. A nod was given, but the permission kept off the records, as no pets are allowed. Reid and a few maintenance men went to work digging a small pothole-sized pit. The men had not been told this was to be an interment for a dog and asked if there was to be a service. None had been planned, but it was clear these men would be upset if at least a prayer wasn't uttered. So Reid made a few impromptu remarks on the life of the deceased, said a prayer and the service ended. The maintenance men commented on what a beautiful service it had been.

Reid's health steadily declined after Jodie's death. He died from a major stroke on April 12, 1997, was cremated and his ashes were placed beside Jodie's. Their graves are near the bell tower. Now they are part of the Oakland tour. Just look for the black marker with the dog sitting on top.

CHAPTER 10

The Famous, Infamous or Should-be Famous

There's one kind favor I'm asking you, asking you, asking you. There's one kind favor
I'm asking you. Please see that my grave's kept clean.
—traditional blues song

THE IRISH TRAVELERS SOCIETY

They've existed in Ireland for hundreds of years as part of the gypsy people and were widely exterminated in World War II, these "tinkers" from Ireland. They detest that name, though it describes their trade specializing in tinsmithing, making pots, cups, funnels, even fiddles. But they seldom cared about the quality of their workmanship, trying to pawn their wares to unsuspecting country folks. The phrase "not worth a tinker's damn" originated from them and their reputation.

During the Irish potato famine years, nearly one million Irish died of malnutrition or disease from the results of poor diets. More than a million fled Ireland, including some of the tinkers. They were the predecessors of America's versions called the Irish Travelers or Irish Horse Traders, nomadic people of the road who meander from town to town, trading horses or selling shoddy wares or services to innocent victims.

They liked the warm climates of the South and settled in Georgia, Tennessee and South Carolina. For many years, April 28 was a most important date, for that was the day they traveled to Atlanta to bury the dead of that year in Oakland Cemetery. The remains had been kept in funeral homes until this date. Like a swarm of ants, the Travelers clan would gather, a funeral mass would be uttered at the Shrine of the Immaculate Conception and then they'd process to Oakland. John McNamara's grave, with a tall angel marking the site, forms the anchor for the Irish Travelers section. After this mass burial, the Travelers would be off.

Father Charles Murphy founded a village for them, named after him, Murphy Village, on the South Carolina–Georgia border, north of Augusta.

John McNamara's grave and angel statue anchor the lot for the Irish Travelers. *Photo by Eric Gaare.*

It's now an incorporated village of some 1,500 or so who live in nice double-wide trailers or in mansions. The women and children stay home now. South Carolina law requires children to go to school through the eighth grade. The men hit the road with false IDs and switch license plates at the first rest stop so their duped customers can't track them down. They return at the end of the school year to pick up the family, and they all hit the road during the summer.

The parents arrange the marriages. No one is allowed to marry outside the clan, which now has only eleven surnames. Mixing at all with outsiders is frowned upon, as this would bring unwanted changes. The Travelers can bring tears to their victims' eyes with sad stories about how the man who ordered all this equipment in their trucks just died from a heart attack and they needed to unload it, and would do so for a song, just so they could get back home to their families. And another sucker is taken in.

They won't squeal on each other, making it hard for the authorities to prosecute. Most of their victims are reluctant to press charges, as no one likes to advertise the fact he's been swindled and made to look the fool. P.T. Barnum said, "There's a sucker born every minute." This is something the Irish Travelers count on.

An investigative police officer once said admiringly that their training at the hands of fathers and uncles was probably as good or better than the training he received as a police official. After all, they spend every day perfecting their craft.

A Traveler would never exploit his own kind, but according to them, the country folk were made to be taken.

GOVERNOR JOHN MARSHALL SLATON: HIS TAKE ON THE LEO FRANK TRIAL

Governor Slaton was thrown into the midst of the notorious Leo Frank/Mary Phagan murder trial when he made the decision of his life—to follow his conscience and commute the death sentence of Leo Frank. It was a political death sentence for him.

For two years following the trial, he received over 100,000 letters from all over the nation—10,000 from Georgia alone—requesting that he either pardon Frank or commute the death sentence to life. The appeal was not going well, so Leo's attorneys came to the governor for a commutation, thinking it was too much to ask for a full pardon. For twelve days Governor Slaton wrestled with the mounds of papers detailing the case and all its discrepancies—the inconsistent testimony of the janitor, Conley; the murder notes written on order pads that had to have come from the basement where the body was found; the strands of hair that did not match Mary Phagan's.

On the morning of June 21, 1915, his wife Sarah asked him if he had reached a decision. His answer was, "It may mean my death or worse, but I have ordered the sentence commuted." She then kissed him and uttered her famous words: "I would rather be the widow of a brave and honorable man than the wife of a coward."

What followed next required all the bravery they could muster. The governor issued a ten-thousand-word statement accompanying his announcement. In private, he told friends he would have issued a full pardon if he had been asked for one. In either case, he bought Frank more time. He said, "Feeling as I do about this case, I would be a murderer if I allowed that man to hang. I would rather be ploughing in a field than to feel for the rest of my life that I had that man's blood in my hands. All I wish now is that the people of Georgia withhold judgment until they have given calm and careful consideration to the statement I have prepared on the case."

But they didn't. Most people were convinced Frank was guilty and called Governor Slaton "the King of the Jews and the Traitor Governor of Georgia." The governor was hanged, shot and burned in effigy. A wave of anti-Semitic demonstrations followed. A crowd of five thousand gathered at city hall to give anti-Slaton speeches, and they burst into the senate chamber at the capitol. A surging mob of two thousand attempted to attack the governor's home on Peachtree Road. The police put up a barricade and enlisted the aid of the state militia. The crowd threw stones and bottles at the police and had to be driven back.

On June 26, 1915, Governor Slaton's last day in office, a mob of two hundred men again attacked his home. He was driven to the inauguration of newly elected Governor Nathaniel E. Harris and was escorted by armed guards. The audience hissed at him. A large man approached the governor, slinging a heavy iron pipe in an assassination attempt, but the would-be assassin was seized by the state militia. Slaton could only think, "Two thousand years ago another governor washed his hands of a case and turned over a Jew to a mob. For two thousand years that governor's name has been accused. If today another Jew were lying in his grave because I had failed to do my duty, I would all through life find his blood on my hands and would consider myself an assassin through cowardice."

Now ex-Governor and Mrs. Slaton escaped to Florida. Leo Frank was transferred for safekeeping from Fulton County jail to the state prison at Milledgeville, one hundred miles away, and the stage was set. Little did John M. Slaton know that his commutation was to cause Leo Frank's death.

Slaton never ran for office again, but continued his work as a lawyer and humanitarian. The day after his death in 1955, Ralph McGill, editor of the *Atlanta Constitution*, wrote, "It was one of destiny's mocking ironies that his great integrity should have cost him his public life." In 1957, the Georgia Legislature erected a monument to Governor Slaton in the state capitol. He was eulogized as the "Incomparable Georgian." President John F. Kennedy included Slaton in his Pulitzer Prize–winning book *Profiles in Courage.*

Governor Slaton is buried in the Grant mausoleum at Oakland, with his wife's family, still living in the shadows over his decision "that we must be measured by our consciences."

George Johnson: Atlanta's Showman

Nearly everyone in Atlanta knew of George Johnson during his sometimes dubious reign as Atlanta's showman from 1850 to 1883. Born in Belfast, Ireland, he immigrated to New York and began his up-and-down career as a showman and circus performer. When the circus traveled south, he fell in love with Augusta and settled there. A big fire in Augusta in 1852 was the first time he lost it all.

Moving to Atlanta, he opened a tent show on Decatur Street and had a successful run. He invested in a successful saloon/hotel. Then came the Civil War. With money still in his pocket, he built Atlanta's first postwar theatre, the Bell Johnson Hall. But the business went bankrupt. So he went back to his showman's roots and bought a sideshow. The *Atlanta Daily Constitution* described it thusly: "George Johnson, the veteran showman with his plank target in the shape of a man, was on hand with this and other games of a like unattractive character." He lost his house and lot over this investment.

Next he opened up a "menagerie" of life-sized stuffed lions and tigers, with a mermaid and a mummy thrown in. One night he was knocked in the head and never fully recovered, physically or financially. One by one his stuffed animal collection disappeared. He was living at a boardinghouse with the following occupants: part-owner Mary Berryman, listed as a lewd woman; James Berryman, Mary's brother and listed as a streetcar driver; Alice Hodges, another lewd woman, and her son Howard; Nora Clayton, another lewd woman; a dressmaker; a painter; a builder; and an attorney. Mary Berryman advertised the boardinghouse as a place where nearly all the services you need are under one roof!

George Johnson died a poor man in 1883 at the age of sixty-two and is buried at Oakland.

ROBERT TYRE JONES: THE GOLFER

Bobby Jones was the first player to win the grand slam of golf: the U.S. Open, the U.S. Amateur, the British Open and the British Amateur, and all in the year 1930 and as an amateur golfer. This feat has never been duplicated. He's buried at Oakland Cemetery. While people who ask for "the Author" at Oakland mean Margaret Mitchell, people who ask for "the Golfer" are immediately taken down the marked path to the gravesite of Robert Tyre Jones and his wife, Mary Malone Jones.

Born on St. Patrick's Day in 1902, Bobby was named for his paternal grandfather, who considered golf to be a complete waste of time. Bob Jones (the name he preferred) described himself as "odd looking with an over-sized head and a spindling body and legs with staring knees and some serious digestive derangements which caused my parents and six or seven doctors a good deal of distress." His first love was baseball, but then he discovered golf and had a swing that was "pure poetry." He was a temperamental player at first, flinging his golf club when a stroke didn't go his way.

When he was tossed out of the British Open in 1921 for his misbehavior, he called this "the most glorious failure of my golfing life," for golf was a sport of manners and a sport for gentlemen. He learned to control his temper enough so that the British said they had "never seen an American like him" and considered him the best that could ever be.

People still talk about his famous lily pad shot at the U.S. Open during his sweep year when his ball skipped across the lake like a skipping stone and landed on the green. When he won the sweep, it took a cordon of fifty marines to safely escort him to the clubhouse and away from the swarming, excited fans. The *New York Times* called it "the most triumphant journey any man ever traveled in sport."

Then Bobby called it quits, saying there was nothing more for him to do. He went home to Atlanta, to his wife and three children, and concentrated on his law practice and supporting his family. Of course he didn't completely quit golf. He designed the one and only Masters golf course in Augusta and played in that tournament through 1948, when the pain and atrophy started. He was diagnosed with syringomyelia, a crippling disease similar to Lou Gehrig's, which causes progressive paralysis but leaves the brain functioning normally. He said that "blessing" allowed him to watch himself slowly deteriorate.

Six days before he died in 1971, to make his long-suffering Catholic wife Mary happy, he converted to Catholicism and was given his last rites. His caddy from St. Andrews, home of the British Open, said of him, "Aye, you're a wonder sir, a blooming wonder."

"The Golfer," Robert Tyre Jones. Note the golf tributes left by fans on their way to the Masters in Augusta. *Photo by Eric Gaare.*

Golfers often pay tribute to him on their way to and from the Masters, leaving signed golf balls or golf tees in front of his modest Oakland tombstone. There are eighteen specimen plants, similar to the ones in Augusta, that line the way to and from his gravesite. You just follow the well-marked signs to his grave.

MARGARET MITCHELL MARSH: THE AUTHOR

People visit Oakland for the sole intent of viewing "the Author's" grave, making a pilgrimage to her. Of course they're talking about Margaret Mitchell, author of "the Book," Atlanta's Civil War tome *Gone with the Wind*. Next to the Bible, it is one of the most widely sold and read books in the world. Today over a quarter-million copies are still sold yearly.

"Peggy" came from a very Southern family. On her father's side were Irish Protestants and her mother's were Irish Catholics, setting the tone for Tara and the indomitable Scarlett O'Hara. Peggy grew up on family stories and Southern stories and stored them away in her author's brain to use in her one grand

"The Author's" grave. Note that she's on the Marsh side, reflecting her married name. Her parents are on the Mitchell side. *Photo by Robert Gaare.*

novel. Purportedly her first husband, Red Upshaw, was the prototype for Rhett Butler. Her second husband, John Marsh, was the model for Ashley Wilkes, and Dr. D'Alvigny was the model for Dr. Meade. An aunt once said to Peggy, "There are just two kinds of people, wheat people and buckwheat people. But buckwheat yields to the wind, is flattened, but when the wind passes, it rises up just as straight as ever." There you have *Gone with the Wind* in a nutshell.

In the 1920s in Atlanta, Peggy was famous for her daring apache dance and her short flapper dresses that showed off her legs. She got thrown out of the Junior League for her daring behavior. But they took her back after her book turned out to be golden. She never owned a house, instead living in an apartment she called "the Dump." This way she would get out of having to repay dinner invitations, telling friends her place was a dump and hardly an appropriate setting for eating lovely meals.

The cabdriver who ran her down on August 11, 1949, served three months' jail time. That night he was driving to get medicine for his family. Peggy was short and tiny, and he didn't see her dart out to cross the street. Her family asked for leniency for him. It was an accident, after all.

For years after her death, her publisher sent tulip bulbs to plant at her gravesite. Frankly my dear, people do give a damn.

DR. ALBERT HAPE: THE AIR BALLOON AGE COMES TO ATLANTA

Daredevil dentist Dr. Albert Hape, along with Professor Samuel A. King and his hot air balloon the *Hyperion*, took to the Atlanta skies on December 10, 1869. It was an event that attracted a crowd of six thousand, peering from windows and rooftops and lining the State Road. Prior to the launch of the *Hyperion*, balloons shaped like fish, elephants, seals, dogs and people were let loose, to the amusement of the crowd. Then Dr. Hape and Professor King got into the basket of their gas-filled balloon and took off in a northwestwardly direction.

The winds shifted and they floated northeast, reaching a height of one mile. For about half an hour they could be seen. Amusing anecdotes sprung from the awe-struck crowd: "If that Dr. Hape owes you anything, you better forget it…they're nearer heaven now than they'll ever get…This must be a new way for revenue officers to hunt for hidden stills." While aloft, Professor King played some pieces on his bugle. When the balloon passed near a tent revival, one woman shouted, "That's Gabriel blowing his horn. The world's coming to an end and I thank God I lived to see this."

But eventually they had to come down, and hopefully before dark. To hasten their descent, they lightened the load, throwing overboard everything that could be spared: wine bottles, sandbags, even the bugle. Then they hit a tree, bounced thirty feet or more and landed safely in Lindsay Peak's cotton field, twenty-six miles from Marietta.

The two announced they would make a second flight a few weeks later on New Year's Day. Professor King changed his mind at the last minute, thinking that conditions weren't right for a launch and the balloon wasn't safe. The undaunted Dr. Hape, who perhaps had more showman in him than George Johnson, cut the ropes and launched himself solo.

When it was a mile or so in the air, the balloon exploded and collapsed in midair. The crowd was horrified. This surely must be the end of Dr. Albert Hape. But an hour or so later, he rode into town on a horse, unscathed from his terrifying fall. In true heroic manner, he had made a parachute of the torn balloon canvas and landed safely, although a bit shaken.

He was like a cat with nine lives. During the Civil War he had been left for dead at Griswoldville, the only battle during Sherman's march, where old men and young boys faced Sherman's finest. It was suicide for the Rebels. He recovered, living with only one functioning lung.

His nine lives were used up at the age of only forty-three, when he died of heart failure in 1884. His brother, Dr. Samuel Hape, also a dentist, but less of a daredevil, is credited with founding the town of Hapeville, Georgia, which bears his name. Albert, Samuel and his family are buried at Oakland in a very choice location near the bell tower.

JASPER NEWTON SMITH: OAKLAND'S WATCHMAN

Perhaps the most colorful resident at Oakland is Jasper Newton Smith, whose life-sized sculpture sits atop his mausoleum close to the entrance of Oakland.

Living in Georgia from 1833 until his death in 1918, Jasper was described as "strictly an original and will pass into history as one of the few originals who ever lived. When nature molded him, she broke the die." Born in rural Georgia, he was a self-made man who could barely read and write, but he was a shrewd businessman. He set up a brick business in Atlanta while the city lay in ruins. He sold millions of bricks as the city was rebuilt and used the money to invest in real estate and to build two landmark buildings in downtown Atlanta.

One of these buildings was known as "the House that Jack Built," on the corner of Peachtree and Carnegie Way. When the city tore it down, they had to honor a promise to Jasper to keep the building's original cornerstone. Supposedly it contains Bible verses that point out the importance of good economy. His second building was known as "the Bachelor's Domain," a residence for men only, with each apartment named after a state of the Union and decorated with a coat of arms and scenes from the history of that state. Saying you lived in Delaware took on a different meaning at the Bachelor's Domain. House rules prevented any guest from allowing a woman to enter, but after Jasper's two daughters and son married and moved in, he turned the Bachelor's Domain into a regular hotel. He and his wife moved in too.

There's an interesting story told about Jasper and his older daughter, Anna. Thomas Jefferson Donaldson, a protégé of Jasper's who worked for him at the Department of Public Works in Fulton County, often came over to the Smith house to play cards with Jasper. Once Jasper made a bet that if Donaldson won the card game, he'd give him one of his daughters. Donaldson won and claimed Anna, who was only three at the time. He married her fifteen years later, when she was a proper eighteen and he was thirty-two.

The most oft-told stories of Jasper have to do with a portrait of him and the mausoleum statue. Both involve the wearing of neckties. As a young boy, Jasper nearly choked to death when he was caught in a vine, which gave him a lifelong phobia against anything tight around his neck, especially neckties. When he commissioned a local artist to paint his portrait to hang

Eccentric Jasper Newton Smith, hat in hand, greeting or frowning upon visitors to Oakland as they enter the front gates. *Photo by Eric Gaare.*

in the entranceway of the family home, the artist painted in a necktie, as it was the fashion of the day for men to wear one. Jasper refused to accept or pay for the painting. The artist painted it out, but Jasper still refused the painting, saying she had desecrated his character by putting a piece of ribbon around his neck. On the way home he stopped at the homeplace and realized the portrait of him was perfect for display in the front hall. He told one of his daughters she could go back to the artist's studio and offer the artist $100 (although the original price had been much more). The artist gladly accepted the offer, since no one else would want to buy the painting, and the portrait was brought home to hang in the front hall. For these types of transactions he was known as a most astute businessman.

The other oft-told tale, and one very similar in nature, has to do with the life-sized sculpture he commissioned from sculptor Oliver W. Edwards to sit atop his Oakland mausoleum. The story goes that Edwards carved in a tie, not knowing of Jasper's aversion to them, and Smith again refused to pay. Sculptor and model haggled for two years before Edwards relented and chipped away the tie. However, in a 1982 letter to the editor of the *Atlanta Journal-Constitution*, Edwards's daughter, J. Coalie Edwards of Duluth, disputed the story. She says her father made a plaster model to go by, which did have a tie on it. Mr. Smith broke it with his cane and then sat in a chair while her father measured his features and then carved the statue. Mr. Smith accepted it without complaint.

And there he sits, forever and ever, in his favorite chair, top hat on his lap and of course tieless, watching the comings and goings at Oakland. He's the only Smith family member who resides at the mausoleum, a true Atlanta eccentric and a favorite stop on any Oakland tour.

CHAPTER 11

Those Who Died Too Young

Dear child thy pure life's cadence—
A sad, yet sweet, refrain—
Shall wake the hearts now broken
To life and hope again—
And fall a benediction
When at the day's decline,
Pale sorrow lowly bending
Weeps at affection's shrine.
—From "In Memoriam, to a Child Who Drowned," Joel Chandler Harris

THE BLOOMFIELD GIRLS

The saddest sightings at Oakland are over the numerous graves of infants and children who died too soon, too early. Joel Chandler Harris himself experienced the death of two grandsons, who are buried at Oakland. One of the most tragic stories of infant deaths is the story of the four Bloomfield girls. The father, Michael, came from Queens County, Ireland. He and his wife Elizabeth produced four beautiful girls: Bridget, born in 1855; Anna, in 1857; Catherine, in 1859; and Isabella, in 1861. They were born in two-year intervals and died within nine days of each other. It was 1863, and the cause of death was likely diphtheria, possibly smallpox, as there were epidemics of both at that time. They passed away slightly out of order. Anna, six, died first on January 11; Bridget, eight, died second on January 13; Catherine, four, died on January 17; and Isabella, two, died on January 20. The grief from this tragedy is hard to fathom. There's a beautiful monument erected by the family in their honor. But more poignant are the small headstones where their individual graves are located. The only stones left intact are Isabella's and Catherine's. Bridget's and Anna's have broken off, leaving only small pieces to represent their brief lives.

Isabella and Catherine Bloomfield, two of the four Bloomfield daughters that died within nine days of each other in 1863. Bridget and Anna's markers are no longer there. *Photo by Eric Gaare.*

JENNIE AND ROSA ROY

Near Herman Benjamin's plot is the memorial to the Roy twins, Jennie (Virginia Taylor) and Rosa (Rosa Garnett), twin sisters who died within two weeks of each other. They died apart, however. Jennie died in Atlanta and Rosa in Richmond, but they died of the same disease—typhoid fever. They were only sixteen. They were the daughters of Dr. G.G. and Flora Roy, and they died in July of 1878. Their marker is very weathered, making it difficult to read, but it says, "Twins in birth, twins in life, twins in the grave, and twins in Heaven. May we be ready too." They are buried side by side.

CHARLIE SANDERS HEMPHILL

Charlie Sanders Hemphill was only two and a half years old when he died. At the memorial service, his little brother said "must wake," but of course he did not. A newspaper memoriam, probably written by a family member, spoke most eloquently of his death on October 21, 1876, and the effect of

117

Charlie Sanders Hemphill died in 1876 at the age of two and a half and is one of Oakland's infants. *Photo by Robert Gaare.*

"Our Charlie" on the family. These words also speak of how universally difficult it is for any parent to lose one so young. I reprint part of that memoriam here:

> *Little Charlie comes back no more unless in the shape of a viewless messenger through the viewless winds to whisper father and mother on and up. Therefore it was hard to let him go,—not that in our selfishness we could bring him back, but because he was so dear and we shall miss him so. His bright mind, his affectionate disposition, and his generous nature that would always divide even to the half of what he had, won the love of friends as well as parents. The absence of his merry greeting, of the pattering of his tiny feet as he ran to meet you or cheerily to do your bidding, will leave an "aching void." And so sorrow we must.*

Three Special Tributes

The seventy thousand plus souls who reside within Oakland's walls, and the stories they have to tell, keep me coming back time and time again.
—Mary Woodlan, Oakland volunteer manager

PETER AND ANNETTE MAYFIELD

N ext to the Waid Hill mausoleum, the plainest at Oakland, one can't help but notice a beautifully kept and lovingly cared for plot, with a bench for repose, arched monument, blooming seasonal flowers and neatly landscaped paths leading the way to the various graves. This is a description of the twenty gravesites of the ancestors of Peter Mayfield, the fourth-generation descendant of the original deed owner Winston Woods and his wife, Mary Ann Grubbs Wood.

Winston purchased the lot in 1872 and upon his death, willed the lot to be passed down to the eldest daughter in each generation. Eventually the lot passed down to Peter's mother's generation. She had two sisters, Ada Minor and Annie Ruth, who died before his mother, so the plot was eventually passed down to her. Peter being an only child, the lot is currently deeded to him. When it fell into his hands, it was in disrepair and had been neglected for years.

In 2005, Annette Mayfield, Peter's wife, discovered she had breast cancer. Her illness helped them decide to take action on the old family plot. They had just sold their house of many years, downsizing to a condominium. Annette, an avid gardener, was looking for a new gardening project and there it was—the old family plot at Oakland. The two hired a landscaping crew to help with the initial cleanup, but they tend the lot themselves, every weekend, when weather permits. The trunk of their car is filled with rakes, hoes, clippers, gloves and trowels.

Of the remaining spots on the family lot, there is one space left for a full-sized grave. Their daughter will take that spot. Her husband will be

The peaceful, well-kept gravesite of the ancestors of Peter Mayfield is one of the best examples of loving, perpetual care at Oakland. Dotted with seasonal flowers, it looks attractive year-round. *Photo by Robert Gaare.*

cremated and will fit into a border space. Annette and Peter will also be cremated and join their son-in-law in border spaces. Their family name, Mayfield, will be engraved onto the bench, the focal point of the garden.

They will eventually join the company of relatives unknown from long ago, as well as five unknown Confederate soldiers thought to have been buried on their site. When space was needed during the Civil War for the ever-growing war dead, families gave up open plots.

Annette's cancer is currently in remission.

FRANKLIN AND FRANCES GARRETT

Franklin Miller Garrett, who died March 5, 2000, at the age of ninety-three, was the foremost authority on the city of Atlanta and surrounding areas. A native of Milwaukee, he moved to Atlanta as a boy and declared his new city forevermore his adopted hometown.

As a boy, he had a fascination with cemeteries and was known to set out on his bicycle to cover a thirty-mile radius around Atlanta, transcribing

Franklin Miller Garrett, Atlanta's unofficial historian, buried in this prominent spot by the entrance walk and guard house. His wife Frances is buried beside him. *Photo by Eric Gaare.*

inscriptions off tombstones in all the cemeteries inside that circle. Mother Nature and Father Time might have worn off inscriptions so that they can't be read today, but Franklin Garrett's cemetery rubbings from his boyhood can be read and serve as priceless records of what might have otherwise been lost forever.

Franklin was the youngest member of the Atlanta Historical Society when he joined in 1927 at the age of twenty-one and eventually concluded his extensively detailed two-volume history, *Atlanta and Environs: A Chronicle of Its People and Events*, an invaluable work that I turned to many times to double-check facts and data for this book.

There was once a *Stump Franklin Garrett* radio show, in which callers could try to ask some outlandishly obscure question to see if they could stump the awesome, fact-filled mind of Mr. Garrett. A caller once asked, "Who was the elevator operator at Dinkler Plaza in 1945?" Franklin's answer was, "Which shift?" (The Dinkler Hotel was the home of Atlanta's Playboy Club, where celebrities like Dean Martin entertained. It was well known for the blinking-eyed owls on top of the columns and was one of the top socialite hotels in the city until it was demolished in 1973. I had to look up this information. It would have been a no-brainer for Franklin Garrett.)

As Franklin grew older, his memory had a few fuzzy spots, or his mind would wander off on some tangent. His devoted wife, Frances, would gently steer him back onto the subject at hand. Frances, whose list of accomplishments rivals that of her husband, died in 2005. The two are buried side by side at Oakland in the north public grounds by the guardhouse.

BETTY SHERWOOD

Elizabeth Jones Sherwood, who died on April 23, 2004, was the quintessential Oakland tour guide for fifteen years and my first introduction to Historic Oakland Cemetery.

I'd been told she was the tour guide to ask for, and luckily she was available to take my Girl Scout troop in 1994 on a trip into Atlanta's past. In her soft Southern drawl, she entertained us with stories of Tweet, the mockingbird pet of Frederica Weimer who is buried in his own grave at Oakland; "the Author," Margaret Mitchell, of the book we all couldn't put down; and the sad story of the four Bloomfield girls who died within nine days of each other at the ages of two, four, six and eight.

Betty was once quoted as saying, "Oakland is the place to come and stop and reassess and carry those things with you. I come because I love the atmosphere. I love to remember."

Now she too is part of those things to be remembered. Betty was cremated, with half of her ashes at Oakland and the other half with her parents at Westview Cemetery. Her daughter, Liz Weaver, the fifth of six generations of Elizabeths, says she hopes it is her mother's legs and mouth that are at Oakland.

Sperry M. Wilder, a current tour guide and expert on the women of Oakland, says, "I learned from the best. Veteran tour guide Betty Sherwood was my mentor. Today she's the first stop on my Women of Oakland Tour. I dedicate everything I do at Oakland to Betty, and if you ever see me sitting in this one spot talking to a bush, I'm not crazy and I'm not Moses. I'm talking to Betty."

Elizabeth Jones Sherwood wrote the Oakland newsletter for many years and was described by famous Atlanta author and columnist Celestine Sibley as a gifted essayist and poet, "the writer with the Midas touch."

Epilogue

Oakland is Atlanta's last tangible link to its past. There are very few places in Atlanta that you can see and say, "That was here in 1850." Oakland tells the story of the history of the people of Atlanta, and it is therefore necessary that this place and its stories be preserved for future generations.

There is a sense of urgency, I feel, that we restore and promote Historic Oakland so that it will be relevant today and in the future. Because it is truly a living history, providing Atlanta a look at how its past has shaped its future, we are not just renovating. We are teaching. We are teaching about the past with an eye on the future. Visitors, while touring the cemetery, can view Atlanta's vibrant skyline while standing on the graves of the people who created it. It is a living history.

David Moore
Executive Director
Historic Oakland Foundation

The mission of the Historic Oakland Foundation is to assist the city of Atlanta with the restoration, preservation and beautification of the cemetery and to promote it as a local cultural resource and a historic site of national importance.

Historic Oakland Cemetery is a city of Atlanta public park; however, the Historic Oakland Foundation exists to perform the much-needed restoration and preservation of the hardscapes (monuments and mausoleums) for which the city is unable to allocate resources. The operating cash flow that goes to restoration comes from support of the community in the form of donations, memberships, foundation grants and revenue from tours and special event promotions.

The main entrance to Oakland. Jasper Newton Smith's shoes can be seen far right. *Photo by Eric Gaare.*

Donations to help preserve Historic Oakland Cemetery can be sent to:
Historic Oakland Foundation
248 Oakland Avenue SE
Atlanta, GA 30312

In death, these Oakland souls remain a living part of us all, our heritage, our roots, our foundations. Their stories are our stories. We are not complete without them. What a privilege it was to tell some of the tales in this book. To all the speaking stones of Oakland I leave this blessing:

> *Warm summer sun shine brightly here,*
> *Soft summer wind blow lightly here,*
> *Sweet sod above, lie light, lie light,*
> *Good night, dear heart, good night.*

Cathy Kaemmerlen

Bibliography

Atlanta Journal-Constitution. www.AJC.com/archives.

Boylston, Elise Reid. *Atlanta: Its Lore, Legends, and Laughter*. Doraville, GA: Foote & Davies, 1968.

Criswell, George, and Ginger Criswell. *This Is History: Atlanta's Oakland Cemetery*. DVD documentary. Atlanta: Criswell Productions, 2000.

Ellis, L.B. "Logan E. Bleckley, Former Chief Justice of the Supreme Court of Georgia." *The Green Bag* 9, no. 5. Arlington, VA: George Mason University, November 1903.

Ferguson, Scott. "Silent Lessons from Oakland's Forgotten: Potter's Field." *Atlanta Magazine*, May 1980.

Frederick, Allen. *Secret Formula.* NY: Harper Collins Books, 1994.

Garrett, Franklin M. *Atlanta and Environs: A Chronicle of Its People and Events.* Vols. 1 and 11. Athens: University of Georgia Press, 1969.

———. *Yesterday's Atlanta*. Miami: E.A. Seemann Pub., 1974.

Harris, Julia Collier. *Life and Letters of Joel Chandler Harris*. Boston: Houghton Mifflin Co., 1918.

Henderson, Dr. Alexa Benson. "Atlanta's Black Heritage." *Atlanta Historical Bulletin* (September 1977). Edited by Franklin Garrett.

Bibliography

————. "Paupers Pastors and Politicians: Reflections Upon Afro-Americans Buried in Oakland Cemetery." *Atlanta Historical Bulletins* 20, no. 2 (Summer 1976).

Interviews with Peter and Annette Mayfield, Patricia Scheff, Susan B. Deaver, Penny Hart and Pat McClure, February–May 2007.

Journal of Negro History 64, no. 4 (Autumn 1979): 395–97.

Knight, Lucian Lamar. *Georgia's Landmarks, Memorials and Legends.* Vols. 1 and 2. Atlanta: Byrd Printing Co., 1914.

Ladies Memorial Association Papers. MSS #375, Boxes 1 and 8. Kenan Research Center, Atlanta History Center Archives.

————. MSS #375.2, Box 1. E. Kenan Research Center, Atlanta History Center Archives.

Mason, Herman "Skip," Jr. *Black Atlanta in the Roaring Twenties: Images of America Series.* Charleston, SC: Arcadia Publishing, 1997.

Newspaper Archive. www.newspaperarchive.com.

Oakland Cemetery Papers, Boxes 1–4. E. Kenan Research Center, Atlanta History Center Archives.

Oney, Steve. *And the Dead Shall Rise: The Murder of Mary Phagan and the Lynching of Leo Frank.* NY: Vintage Press, 2003.

Park, Hugh. "The Blacks in Oakland." *Atlanta Journal,* September 9, 1976.

Reed, Thomas Walter. "Logan Edwin Bleckley and FDR." Chap. 18 in *History of University of Georgia.* Self-published, 1935.

Russell, James Michael. *Atlanta: 1847-1890: City Building in the Old South and the New.* Baton Rouge: Louisiana State University Press, 1988.

Salyer, Sharon L. "Oakland: City's Most Tangible tie to 131 Years of Its History." *Atlanta Constitution,* September 21, 1981.

Bibliography

Shavin, Norman. *Old Atlanta: An Exercise in Nostalgia*. Atlanta: Century House, 1969.

Sibley, Celestine. *Peachtree Street, USA*. NY: Doubleday and Co., 1963.

Smith, George Gilman, D.P. "Recollections of an Atlanta Boy: 1847–1855." *Atlanta Journal*, 1909.

Taliaferro, Tevi. *Images of America: Historic Oakland Cemetery*. Charleston, SC: Arcadia Press, 2001.

Windham, Donald. *Emblems of Conduct*. Athens: University of Georgia Press, 1996.

Yarbrough, Cathy. "History Buried Here: City's Famous/Forgotten in Oakland Cemetery." *Atlanta Constitution*, April 12, 1973.

Zaworski, Dr. Robert E. *Confederate Sections at Oakland Cemetery, Atlanta, Georgia, History and Restoration*. Vols. 1 and 2. Self-published, 1996.

———. *Headstones of Heroes—Restoration and History of Confederate Graves in Atlanta's Oakland Cemetery*. Paducah, KY: Turner Pub. Co., 1998.

About the Author

Cathy Kaemmerlen is a professional actress, dancer, playwright and storyteller known for her variety of one-woman shows and characters. She has developed and performs over thirty in-school programs and her multiple living history shows on various periods of American history, concentrating on the Civil War. A collector of stories, she has traveled and toured widely under the auspices of Young Audiences, the National Women's History Project and the Georgia and South Carolina Arts Commissions. A Hambidge fellow for over ten years (where she writes many of her shows), and featured artist on the Southern Artist Profile of the Southern Arts Exchange, she has produced two storytelling CDs: *Foolish Folk* and *New Manchester Girl*. She published her first book, *General Sherman and the Georgia Belles*, with The History Press in 2006.

Cathy is Southern born and bred to Yankee parents and is the proud mother of three—Michael (twenty-five), Sara (twenty-three) and Eric (twenty-one)—and wife to Robert Gaare, who owns his own printing business in Marietta, Georgia.

Check her out at www.tattlingtales.com.